At Issue

Adaptation and Climate Change

Other Books in the At Issue Series:

Are Adoption Policies Fair?

Are Players' Unions Good for Professional Sports Leagues?

Biofuels

Cancer

Do Schools Prepare Students for a Global Economy?

Do Veterans Receive Adequate Health Care?

Food Insecurity

Foreign Oil Dependence

Gay Marriage

Is Selling Body Parts Ethical?

Polygamy

Should Parents Choose the Sex of Their Children?

Should the Legal Drinking Age Be Lowered?

Solar Storms

Technology and the Cloud

Teen Driving

What Is the Role of Technology in Education?

Wikileaks

At Issue

Adaptation and Climate Change

Roman Espejo, Book Editor

GREENHAVEN PRESS
A part of Gale, Cengage Learning

Detroit • New York • San Francisco • New Haven, Conn • Waterville, Maine • London

GALE
CENGAGE Learning·

Elizabeth Des Chenes, *Director, Publishing Solutions*

© 2013 Greenhaven Press, a part of Gale, Cengage Learning

Gale and Greenhaven Press are registered trademarks used herein under license.

For more information, contact:
Greenhaven Press
27500 Drake Rd.
Farmington Hills, MI 48331-3535
Or you can visit our Internet site at gale.cengage.com

For product information and technology assistance, contact us at

Gale Customer Support, 1-800-877-4253
For permission to use material from this text or product, submit all requests online at
www.cengage.com/permissions

Further permissions questions can be emailed to permissionrequest@cengage.com

Articles in Greenhaven Press anthologies are often edited for length to meet page requirements. In addition, original titles of these works are changed to clearly present the main thesis and to explicitly indicate the author's opinion. Every effort is made to ensure that Greenhaven Press accurately reflects the original intent of the authors. Every effort has been made to trace the owners of copyrighted material.

Cover image copyright © Debra Hughes 2007. Used under license from Shutterstock .com.

LIBRARY OF CONGRESS CATALOGING-IN-PUBLICATION DATA

Adaptation and climate change / Roman Espejo, book editor.
    p. cm. -- (At issue)
    Includes bibliographical references and index.
    ISBN 978-0-7377-6141-2 (hardcover) -- ISBN 978-0-7377-6142-9 (pbk.)
    1. Climatic changes. 2. Climatic changes--Environmental aspects. 3. Climate change mitigation. 4. Global environmental change. I. Espejo, Roman, 1977-
    QC902.9.A33 2012
    577.2'2--dc23

                                                              2012024913

Printed in the United States of America
1 2 3 4 5   16 15 14 13 12

Contents

Introduction

Green consumerism "simply means that individuals have the opportunity and desire to consider environmental impacts when making purchases and other everyday choices,"[1] says Tom Watson, project manager for King County's Recycling and Environmental Services in Washington, in the *Seattle Times*. He credits small businesses and grassroots organizations for spurring the developments and innovations that have increased the availability and range of eco-friendly products, from organic food to sustainable building materials. "Currently, however, large corporations such as Home Depot, Ford, and General Electric are driving the green-consumerism bus in this country," Watson maintains. "Much of that corporate influence is positive, because large companies do help make green products more available to the public," he adds.

Advocates of buying green contend that it is an effective way for consumers to respond to climate change, but is not practiced enough. "The destruction of nonrenewable resources, global warming, industrial toxins that are polluting water, our bodies, soil—all of it is due to us, but we don't see the connection ordinarily between what we buy and the actual ecological damage done along the way during the life cycle of that product,"[2] asserts Daniel Goleman, author of *Ecological Intelligence: How Knowing the Hidden Impacts of What We Buy Can Change Everything*, in a *Newsweek* interview. According to Goleman, more than 80,000 industrial chemicals are found in everyday items, and many of these have been determined as being toxic to humans and the environment. "Once we know the truth, then that information becomes a guide to smarter

1. April 20, 2012 http://seattletimes.nwsource.com/html/ecoconsumer/2018003155
   _ecoconsumer21m.html
2. July 20, 2009 http://www.thedailybeast.com/newsweek/2009/07/20/it-s-not-easy
   -buying-green.html

buying—to buying that minimizes the danger to ourselves and our loved ones and to our planet," Goleman insists.

Shoppers are also urged to swap conventional goods for their sustainable alternatives. For example, environmental nonprofit Green America singles out paper products as one of the things that should always contain post-consumer content: "38.9 percent of waste in the average American household is paper. Paper made from virgin materials contributes to deforestation and global warming, and often ends up taking up landfill space."[3] In fact, some believe that all consumer choices have an effect, no matter how small. "It's tempting to think that the scale of the challenge means there's simply nothing we as individuals can do,"[4] writes green consultant and entrepreneur Julia Hailes in her book *The New Green Consumer Guide*. "But if millions of people make changes—even relatively minor ones—the impact is enormous."

Nonetheless, even as it becomes mainstream, green consumerism faces vocal criticism in mitigating and adapting to climate change. According to Gernot Wagner, an economist at the Environmental Defense Fund, shopping sustainably is not enough to make a difference. "Just know that it won't save the tuna, protect the rain forest, or stop global warming. The changes necessary are so large and profound that they are beyond the reach of individual action,"[5] he states in a *New York Times* op-ed. Wagner claims that yearly emissions must be cut in half at the minimum by the year 2050—a strategy that still will not prevent the catastrophic effects of climate change. "The reality is that we cannot overcome the global threats posed by greenhouse gases without speaking the ultimate in-

3. greenamerica.org (accessed May 14, 2012) http://www.greenamerica.org/programs/shopunshop/buyinggreen/whattobuy.cfm
4. London, UK: Simon & Schuster, 2007.
5. September 7, 2011. http://www.nytimes.com/2011/09/08/opinion/going-green-but-getting-nowhere.html

convenient truth: getting people excited about making individual environmental sacrifices is doomed to fail," Wagner concludes.

Others suggest that buying green can actually be counterproductive and encourage consumers to make decisions that are not eco-friendly. In a 2010 study, participants who purchased green products were more prone to lying and stealing than those who chose other products. "While mere exposure to green products can have a positive societal effect by inducing pro-social and ethical acts, purchasing green products may license indulgence in self-interested and unethical behaviors,"[6] observe Nina Mazar and Chen-Bo Zhong, the Canadian psychologists who conducted the research. In fact, some argue that sustainable goods, even if they are better for the environment, do not solve the problem of consumerism itself. "As positive as it is that more people want to be green shoppers, the truth is that green consumerism can inadvertently contribute to the problem of over-consumption, because it encourages people to simply switch brands rather than to ask the more fundamental question: do I really want or need this?"[7] propose Donna Green and Liz Minchin in their book, *Screw Light Bulbs: Smarter Ways to Save Australians Time and Money*.

Buying green is one of the ways people act on climate change in their daily lives. Much more extreme adaptations, such as the relocation of populations from coastal areas due to rising sea levels or preparing for major meteorological changes and disastrous events around the world, are global-warming forecasts that draw as much urgency as they do controversy. The viewpoints in *At Issue: Adaptation and Climate Change* investigates the issues, predictions, and debates surrounding the future of the environment and its inhabitants.

6. "Do Green Products Make Us Better People?" 2010 http://www.rotman.utoronto.ca/facbios/file/Green%20Products%20Psych%20Sci.pdf
7. Perth, AU: University of Western Australia Press, 2010.

1

Climate Change Could Be Devastating and People Must Adapt to Survive

Patrick Gonzalez

Patrick Gonzalez is a forest ecologist and climate-change scientist at the National Park Service.

Scientific evidence demonstrates that increased man-made carbon emissions are linked to global warming, harming ecosystems, and human welfare. Warmer conditions are related to a range of impacts occurring around the world; rising sea levels are displacing coastal communities, and altered seasonal patterns are increasing heat-related deaths and influencing pest infestations as well as affecting agriculture and food security. Therefore, it is urgent that humans act to reduce carbon emissions and take adaptation measures, from enhancing energy efficiency and adjusting crop production to restoring wetlands and relocating populations. Human health can also be protected through improving sanitation, protecting water supplies, and monitoring and controlling disease.

Climate change emerges from the smokestacks and tailpipes of industrial society and ends up as drifting sand surrounding African villages and rising tides flooding Pacific islands. Scientific evidence shows that emissions from automobiles, power plants, and deforestation are causing the Earth to

Patrick Gonzalez, "A World Vulnerable to Climate Change," *WorldView*, Summer 2008, pp. 6–9. Copyright © 2008 by the Carnegie Council for Ethics in International Affairs. All rights reserved. Reproduced by permission.

warm and that the warming is damaging ecosystems and human well-being. Yet, the world can avoid the worst impacts by improving the efficiency of energy use and by conserving forests.

These are the conclusions of the Intergovernmental Panel on Climate Change (IPCC), a group of thousands of scientists convened by the United Nations that conducts the definitive global assessments of climate change. In recognition of this work, the Nobel Committee awarded a share of the 2007 Nobel Peace Prize to the IPCC, with the other share awarded to former Vice President Al Gore.

The world's 6.5 billion people pump into the Earth's atmosphere twice the amount of carbon dioxide than the world's forests and oceans can naturally absorb. The remaining carbon dioxide stays in the atmosphere and traps heat in a phenomenon known as the Greenhouse Effect. Human activities have raised the atmospheric concentration of carbon dioxide to its highest level in 650,000 years. The accumulation of greenhouse gases has raised global temperatures to their warmest levels in 500 to 1,300 years.

Impacts Occurring Now

We are now observing widespread changes to our world that the IPCC attributes to global warming. Warmer conditions have melted arctic sea ice 20% from 1979 to 2006 and melted 2.3-5.7 trillion tons of ice from glaciers and ice caps around the world. Reduced stream flow from glaciers has increased pressure on limited water reservoirs in the Andes. Warmer seas have caused coral bleaching and extensive death of coral reefs in the Caribbean and the South Pacific. Warmer seas have also increased the proportion of Atlantic hurricanes in the most intense categories since 1970, leading to notable storm damage in Mexico, the U.S. and the Caribbean. Global sea level rose 12-22 cm in the 20th Century, pushing some people in Kiribati, the Maldives, Papua New Guinea and the Solomon Islands to migrate away from coastal communities.

Warmer temperatures and changing rainfall are beginning to shift vegetation zones towards polar and equatorial regions and up mountain slopes. In the African Sahel, climate change and desertification have caused the extensive dieback of trees, exposed sandy soils to wind erosion, and shifted the vast ecological zones of the Sahel, Sudan and Guinea southward towards the Equator. The alteration of seasons has changed the timing of life cycle events of plants and animals. Climate change has lifted the cloud deck in the montane forests of Costa Rica, causing a fungus infection that has driven 75 amphibian species to extinction.

An increase in the frequency of relatively hot days and hot nights has increased the number of heat-related deaths of susceptible people around the world. Warmer and wetter conditions have also altered the distribution of forest and agricultural pests, ticks and other vectors of human disease. Agricultural production has demonstrated vulnerability to increased frequency of extreme weather events, contributing to food insecurity.

Changes in the timing of snow melt and increased frequency of extreme storms and droughts may severely reduce freshwater availability for up to a billion people.

Projected Changes in Africa, Asia and Latin America

IPCC projections indicate that continued emission of greenhouse gases may increase temperatures 1.8 to 4° C and raise sea level 18 to 59 cm by the year 2100 a.d., causing more serious damage to ecosystems and people. Those in the weakest economic positions are the most vulnerable to climate change due to lower capacities to adapt to drastic changes.

In Africa, IPCC projects that climate change may increase drought and change growing seasons to an extent that would reduce rain-fed agricultural yields by half in the next two decades. At the same time, climate change could severely reduce the drinking water supplies of up to a quarter billion people. Shifts in vegetation zones may increase the proportion of arid and semi-arid land. Together, all of these changes would exacerbate food insecurity for many people and perhaps aggravate conflict and war. Although it is possible that climate change may expand the range of malaria-carrying mosquitoes, the question of whether climate change will increase or decrease the incidence of malaria in Africa remains unresolved.

In Asia, IPCC projects that rising sea level will threaten millions of people in the Ganges, Brahmaputra and Mekong River deltas with inundation, from rising seas on one side and from flooding rivers on the other. Flooding may reduce the extent of protective mangrove forests while seawater intrusion may degrade freshwater fisheries in river deltas. Warmer temperatures seem to be reducing rice yields in the Philippines, a trend that may continue across Southeast Asia rice areas under continued climate change. Changes in the timing of snow melt and increased frequency, of extreme storms and droughts may severely reduce freshwater availability for up to a billion people. It is possible that climate change will extend the increase in forest fires observed in northern Asia and Indonesia, reducing forest cover and the ecosystem services that forests provide. Warmer coastal water temperatures could increase the incidence and toxicity of cholera across South Asia while continuation of the observed increase in heat waves in India would lead to more heat-related deaths.

In Latin America, increased temperature and decreased soil moisture could convert tropical rainforest in eastern Amazonia into savanna.

Warmer sea temperatures will likely continue to increase the intensity of hurricanes in the Caribbean, increase death of

Mesoamerican coral reefs, and alter Pacific fish stocks off Peru and Chile. IPCC projects that tropical glaciers are very likely to disappear from the Andes in two decades, reducing water availability and hydropower generation in Bolivia, Colombia, Ecuador and Peru. Overall, hydrological and population changes may severely reduce freshwater availability for up to 150 million people in the next two decades. Climate change may reduce yields of major food crops and cattle productivity, exacerbating food insecurity for tens of millions of people by 2080 A.D.

On small islands around the world, continued sea level rise will inundate wider areas while storm surges and coastal erosion will threaten vital infrastructure and settlements. IPCC projects that sea level rise will flood port facilities at Suva, Fiji, and Apia, Samoa and roads and airports on many Pacific islands. Projected reductions in rainfall and seawater intrusion may reduce groundwater by a third on many Pacific atolls.

The potential array of negative impacts of climate change ... will strain the abilities of communities that often cannot assure basic services under current conditions.

Reduce Emissions and Adapt

People in Africa and Latin America live with the consequences of greenhouse gas emissions mainly produced on the other side of the world. The United States, with 5% of the world's population, emits a disproportionate share—22%—of the world's greenhouse gas emissions from fossil fuels. Indeed, each person in the U.S. emits twice the amount of greenhouse gases as each person in France, Japan, Switzerland, and other countries with a high standard of material comfort. Therefore, Americans can take action to help stop global warming by improving the efficiency of their use of energy and natural resources.

The world can avert the most drastic impacts of climate change by reducing greenhouse gas emissions through available energy efficiency and conservation practices and by conserving global forests. Nevertheless, the world must take measures to adapt to the impacts of climate change that are already occurring.

Some potential adaptation measures for agriculture and natural resource management include expanded rainwater harvesting, water storage and conservation, adjustment of planting dates and crop varieties, soil erosion control, conservation of potentially less vulnerable areas (known as refugia) for natural ecosystems, restoration of forests through natural regeneration, and monitoring of ecological indicators to detect ongoing change. Adaptation measures against sea level rise include the restoration of wetlands as protection against storm surges and the more drastic options of constructing expensive sea walls or relocating people. Potential adaptation measures for human health include improved sanitation, protection of drinking water, and disease surveillance and control. The potential array of negative impacts of climate change, however, will strain the abilities of communities that often cannot assure basic services under current conditions.

When we take action on climate change, we reduce the impacts on African farmers, Andean livestock herders, South Pacific fishers, and other people around the world who depend on a hospitable climate.

2

The Negative Impact of Climate Change Is Overstated

Marco Evers, Olaf Stampf, and Gerald Traufetter

Based at German news source Spiegel, Marco Evers is a corre-spondent in London, Olaf Stampf is head of science and technol-ogy, and Gerald Traufetter is an editor.

A recent scandal emerging from global warming research reveals that the touted increase in the Earth's temperature driving the debates about fossil fuels and anthropomorphic climate change is based on sloppy analyses and exaggerations. And the alarmist scenarios presented by climatologists will not become realities: sea levels are not rising to catastrophic levels, the frequency of hurricanes is unrelated to climate change, and the advent of "su-perstorms" is unfounded. In fact, computer simulations used to predict temperatures are imprecise, and models for precipitation are unreliable. Global warming may not be stopped, but the im-pacts—depending on the location or observer—may not be all harmful and even beneficial.

Life has become "awful" for Phil Jones. Just a few months ago, he was a man with an enviable reputation: the head of the Climate Research Unit (CRU) at the University of East Anglia in Norwich, England, an expert in his field and the fa-ther of an alarming global temperature curve that apparently showed how the Earth was heating up as a result of anthropo-genic global warming.

Marco Evers, Olaf Stampf, and Gerald Traufetter, "A Superstorm for Global Warming Research," *Spiegel Online*, April 6, 2010. www.spiegel.de. Reproduced by permission.

Those days are now gone.

Nowadays, Jones, who is at the center of the "Climategate" affair involving hacked CRU emails [which prompted Jones to temporarily step down from his position in December 2009], needs medication to fall sleep. He feels a constant tightness in his chest. He takes beta-blockers to help him get through the day. He is gaunt and his skin is pallid. He is 57, but he looks much older. He was at the center of a research scandal that hit him as unexpectedly as a rear-end collision on the highway.

His days are now shaped by investigative commissions at the university and in the British Parliament. He sits on his chair at the hearings, looking miserable, sometimes even trembling. The Internet is full of derisive remarks about him, as well as insults and death threats. "We know where you live," his detractors taunt.

Jones is finished: emotionally, physically and professionally. He has contemplated suicide several times recently, and he says that one of the only things that have kept him from doing it is the desire to watch his five-year-old granddaughter grow up.

'100 Percent Confident'

One of the conclusions of his famous statistical analysis of the world's climate is that the average temperature on Earth rose by 0.166 degrees Celsius [0.299 degrees Fahrenheit] per decade between 1975 and 1998. This, according to Jones, was the clear result of his research and that of many other scientists.

"I am 100 percent confident that the climate has warmed," Jones says imploringly. "I did not manipulate or fabricate any data."

His problem is that the public doesn't trust him anymore. Since unknown hackers secretly copied 1,073 private emails between members of his research team and published them on the Internet, his credibility has been destroyed—and so has that of an entire profession that had based much of its work on his research until now.

Those who have always viewed global warming as a global conspiracy now feel a sense of satisfaction. The so-called climate skeptics feel vindicated, because Jones, in his written correspondence with colleagues, all of them leading members of the climate research community, does not come across as an objective scientist, but rather as an activist or missionary who views "his" data as his personal shrine and is intent on protecting it from the critical eyes of his detractors.

An Entire Branch of Science in Crisis

The Climategate affair is grist for the mills of skeptics, who have gained growing support for their cause, particularly in English-speaking countries. What began with hacked emails in the United Kingdom has mushroomed into a crisis affecting an entire scientific discipline. At its center is an elite and highly influential scientific group, the Intergovernmental Panel on Climate Change (IPCC).

Working on behalf of the United Nations, the scientists organized under IPCC's umbrella—including Phil Jones—regularly prepare prognoses on the Earth's looming greenhouse climate. Without the IPCC reports, governments would not be embroiled in such passionate debate about phasing out the age of oil and coal.

In late 2007, the IPCC was even awarded the Nobel Peace Prize jointly with former US Vice President Al Gore. IPCC Chairman Rajendra Pachauri, as the personification of the world's conscience, accepted the award on behalf of his organization. "Climate change poses novel risks," Pachauri told his audience, saying that the decision to award the prize to the IPCC was "a clarion call for the protection of the earth as it faces the widespread impacts of climate change." He also warned of the risk of not taking action: "Every year of delay implies a commitment to greater climate change in the future."

Sloppy Work

Since then, the IPCC has experienced a dramatic fall from grace. Less than three years after this triumph, more and more mistakes, evidence of sloppy work and exaggerations in the current IPCC report are appearing. They include Jones' disputed temperature curve, the prediction that all Himalayan glaciers would disappear by 2035—which was the result of a simple transposition of numbers—and the supposed increase in natural disasters, for which no source was given.

In mid-March [2010], UN Secretary General Ban Ki Moon slammed on the brakes and appointed a watchdog for the IPCC. The InterAcademy Council, a coalition of 15 national academies of science, will review the work of the IPCC by this fall.

There is already a consensus today that deep-seated reforms are needed at the IPCC. The selection of its authors and reviewers was not sufficiently nonpartisan, there was not enough communication among the working groups, and there were no mechanisms on how to handle errors. . . .

Regaining Lost Trust

German climatologist Hans von Storch now wants to see an independent institution recalculate the temperature curve, and he even suggests that the skeptics be involved in the project. He points out, however, that processing the data will take several years.

"There is no other way to regain the trust that has been lost," he says, "even if I'm certain that the new curve will not look significantly different from the old one."

And if it does? "That would definitely be the worst-case scenario for climatology. We would have to start all over again."

Other central predictions of climatologists, such as that involving a noticeable rise in sea levels, would also have to be reevaluated. How high sea levels will go in the future is already a matter of debate.

No one talks about such nightmare scenarios today. None of the current simulations involves the complete melting of the Antarctic ice sheet.

The Reality of Rising Sea Levels

They could have been scenes from a horror film: New York's skyscrapers jutted out of the ocean like reefs, while cities like Hamburg and Hong Kong, London and Naples had been flooded long ago. Entire countries had been swallowed up in other places. Denmark, the Netherlands and Bangladesh had ceased to exist.

A quarter of a century ago, climatologists grabbed the public's attention with such horrific visions. At the time, the experts calculated that the sea level would rise by more than 60 meters (197 feet) if the greenhouse effect caused all of the Earth's ice to melt.

No one talks about such nightmare scenarios today. None of the current simulations involves the complete melting of the Antarctic ice sheet. On the other hand, hardly any glaciologists doubt that sea levels will be significantly higher along coastlines by the end of the century. But how much higher, exactly? Estimates range from 18 centimeters (7 inches) to 1.90 meters (6' 3").

Hard to Calculate

"Of course, this isn't a satisfactory statement for coastal planners and politicians," admits Peter Lemke, chief climatologist at the Alfred Wegener Institute for Polar and Marine Research in the northern German port city of Bremerhaven. "But we can't sell something as certainty if we don't know exactly what it will be."

The current IPCC report mentions a relatively conservative range of 18 to 59 centimeters [23 inches]. "Most experts consider this estimate to be too small," says Lemke.

Two factors influence the sea level. The first one affects it directly: When water heats, it expands. This warming effect, which can be calculated with relative precision, is expected to cause the sea level to rise by about 22 centimeters [7.8 inches] by 2100.

Another effect that is not as easy to calculate is the melting of mountain glaciers and inland ice in Greenland and Antarctica. Most of the melting today is happening in mountain glaciers, from the Andes to the Himalayas. According to IPCC calculations, this melting activity contributes 0.8 millimeters a year to the rise in sea level. Greenland and Antarctica each contribute another 0.2 millimeters.

Quicker Melting

Meanwhile, satellite observations indicate that the rate at which the ice is melting has increased. Glaciologists speculate that parts of the Western Antarctic and, to a greater extent, Greenland, are melting more quickly than initially assumed.

But many scientists are reluctant to make new predictions, because the inner processes in the gigantic ice caps remain insufficiently understood. Reliable data on the behavior of calving glaciers has only existed for about 10 years. Greenland's glaciers are currently spitting a particularly large amount of ice into the ocean. After such a phase, however, many ice flows become dormant again for a longer period of time.

Lemke, like most of his fellow scientists, expects the sea level to rise by somewhere between half a meter and one meter.

Build dikes or get out of the way—this is the principle coastal residents have applied for years to defend themselves against the forces of nature. In Hamburg in northern Germany, storm surges are now more than half a meter higher than in the 1960s. This is not the result of climate change, however, but of the narrowing of the Elbe River. Nevertheless, the port city is not as threatened as it once was, thanks to improved flood protection.

But storm surges aren't just caused by rising sea levels. Another factor that is at least as important is the wind, which pushes large amounts of water against coastlines.

Can we truly expect to see stormier times in a greenhouse climate?

The Myth of the Monster Storm

Hurricane Katrina had hardly devastated the southern US city of New Orleans five years ago [in 2005] before a "hurricane war" broke out among US scientists. The alarmists, using the rhetoric of fiery sermons, warned that Katrina was only the beginning, and that we would soon see the advent of super-storms of unprecedented fury. Members of the more level-headed camp were vehemently opposed to such predictions and insisted that there was no justification for such fears.

The study concludes with the assessment that "tropical cyclone frequency is likely to either decrease or remain essentially the same."

The dispute escalated when Kevin Trenberth, a climatologist and a lead author of the IPCC report, announced at a press conference at Harvard University that there was a clear relationship between global warming and the increased intensity of hurricane activity. Chris Landsea, a meteorologist with the National Hurricane Center in Miami, was so furious over this unfounded prediction that he withdrew from his participation in the IPCC.

Now the two rivals have reached a surprising truce, and Landsea has largely prevailed with his reassuring assessment.

Last month [in March 2010] Landsea, together with top US hurricane researchers, published a study that finally disproves the supposed link between hurricanes and global warming. The study concludes with the assessment that "tropical cyclone frequency is likely to either decrease or remain essentially the same." Top wind speeds could increase somewhat, says Landsea, but the changes would "not be truly substantial."

Setback for the IPCC

The all-clear signal on the hurricane front is another setback for the IPCC. In keeping with lead author Kevin Trenberth's predictions, the IPCC report warned that there would be more hurricanes in a greenhouse climate. One of the graphs in the IPCC report is particularly mysterious. Without specifying a source, the graph suggestively illustrates how damage caused by extreme weather increases with rising average temperatures.

When hurricane expert Roger Pielke, Jr. of the University of Colorado at Boulder saw the graph, he was appalled. "I would like to discover this sort of relationship myself," he says, "but it simply isn't supported by the facts at the moment."

Pielke tried to find out where the graph had come from. He traced it to the chief scientist at a London firm that performs risk calculations for major insurance companies. The insurance scientist claims that the graph was never meant for publication. How the phantom graph found its way into the IPCC report is still a mystery.

At first, the fear of monster storms seemed easily justified. Scientists conjectured that as the oceans became warmer, hurricanes would accumulate more energy. But, as is so often the case, the truth is more complicated. A specific set of conditions must be present in the atmosphere to allow a hurricane to develop and survive. "Wind shear can destroy a hurricane in an early stage," says Landsea, who flies into storm cells in research aircraft every year. Wind shear, however, is likely to increase in a warmer climate. For this reason, many computer models now even point to a decline in hurricane activity.

'Nothing Will Change'

Hurricanes have in fact increased since the late 1960s, a phenomenon scientists attribute to a natural cycle in ocean currents. The constantly rising insurance claims reported by reinsurance companies are a particularly unreliable indicator. "When you adjust for the growth in new buildings, road and factories being built in hurricane regions, there is no longer any evidence of an upward trend," Pielke explains.

The prognoses for all storms outside the tropical zone are even clearer. There has been a widespread fear that rising temperatures would lead to more and more powerful storms.

On balance, temperature differences on the Earth's surface will decrease, which in turn will even reduce wind speeds—meaning the much-feared monster storms are unlikely to materialize.

But current long-term forecasts offer no evidence of such a trend, especially not in the temperate latitudes. "All computer models show that nothing will change at all outside the tropics," says Jochem Marotzke, director of the Hamburg Max Planck Institute for Meteorology (MPI-M). "In the future, we will see neither more nor stronger storms gathering over our heads."

In a greenhouse climate, only the storm paths in low-pressure zones are likely to change. There will probably be more wind in Scandinavia and less wind in the Mediterranean region. In Central Europe, on the other hand, no noticeable changes are expected.

It is easy to explain, in physical terms, why stormier times do not lie ahead for most of the world's regions. According to the models, the high latitudes will heat up more substantially than the equatorial zones (which also explains why climate change is already so visible in the Arctic regions). On balance, temperature differences on the Earth's surface will decrease, which in turn will even reduce wind speeds—meaning the much-feared monster storms are unlikely to materialize.

Climate Change's Winners and Losers

Even though researchers have been refining their climate models for more than 30 years, there is one natural phenomenon that continues to elude them. "Clouds still pose the biggest problem for us," says Marotzke. "The uncertainties are still very big. This remains the most important issue for us."

It all seems simple enough in theory. When temperatures rise, more moisture evaporates. But does that mean that more clouds form as a result? And if so, do they curb or accelerate global warming?

On their upper surfaces, clouds act like mirrors. They reflect sunlight back into space, thereby cooling the atmosphere. But on their lower surfaces they prevent the heat reflected by the Earth from escaping, and temperatures rise.

Which of the two effects predominates depends on the height and type of clouds. "You just have to look up to see how many different types there are," says US cloud expert Björn Stevens, the new director of the MPI-M. "And each cloud type behaves differently."

'The Jury Is Still Out'

Until now, no one knew exactly which clouds benefit from a greenhouse climate. But the answer to this question determines whether average global temperatures will end up being one degree higher or lower than predicted by today's models, a factor which creates significant uncertainty. "The jury is still out on which direction the pendulum will take," says Stevens.

Despite the enormous uncertainties, there is agreement on at least one issue: Global warming can no longer be stopped.

But would that be as horrific as has been predicted? Does humanity truly face plagues of biblical proportions? Won't a warmer climate also have its benefits? And won't it lead to higher crop yields and more tourism revenues in many places?

The truth probably lies somewhere in the middle. There will undoubtedly be losers, but there will also be winners. Whether global warming is more likely to be harmful or beneficial depends entirely on the location of the observer.

Imprecise Simulations

Unfortunately, the computer simulations that predict the climate of the future are still too imprecise to be able to draw reliable conclusions for each individual country or region. Although it is relatively easy to predict the amount by which average temperatures will probably rise in different parts of the world, the models are still relatively shaky when it comes to precipitation. In fact, the prognoses the different models make are sometimes very contradictory.

Nevertheless, a clear trend is emerging in most simulations. "In places where it already rains a lot today, it will rain even more," says Erich Roeckner, a veteran climatologist who has spent years simulating changes in precipitation in a warmer climate. "And where it's dry today, it'll be even drier in the future."

The common myth that developing countries, the poorest of the poor, will suffer the most as a result of climate change is wrong—at least according to current climate models.

In central Africa, for example, the models predict that hardly anything will change, and precipitation will likely remain constant. And according to most simulations, precipitation could even increase in the drought- and famine-plagued Sahel. "If this turns out to be true," says Roeckner, "it will of course be a surprisingly positive side effect."

Clear Winners of Climate Change

The clear winners are principally the northern regions of the world where it has up until now been too cold and inhospitable. Countries like Canada and Russia can look forward to better harvests and blossoming tourism. The countries bordering the Arctic also hope that the melting of sea ice will enable them to reach previously inaccessible natural resources. For Scandinavians, for example, the only drawback will be a possible guilty conscience over the fact that they are benefiting from climate change.

It will become more arid, however, in many subtropical regions. Industrialized nations, which bear the greatest culpability for global warming, will be most heavily affected. The new drought zones will probably lie in the southern United States and Australia, as well as in South Africa. In Europe, Mediterranean countries like Spain, Italy and Greece will struggle with even drier climates than they already have today.

The clear winners are principally the northern regions of the world where it has up until now been too cold and inhospitable.

A drastic shift could take place in the European tourism business, as climate change heralds bad times for the large tourist developments in southern Spain and good times for hotels along the North Sea and Baltic Sea coasts. "If I had a vacation house on Mallorca," Max Planck scientist Jochem Marotzke jokes, "I would sell it and look for one on (the Baltic Sea island of) Usedom."

3

Climate Change Will Force the Relocation of Populations

Oli Brown

Oli Brown is a program manager and senior researcher for Trade and Investment and Security programs at the International Institute for Sustainable Development (IISD), a public-policy research institute headquartered in Winnipeg, Canada.

Global temperatures were projected to rise dramatically by 2099. As areas of dry land, droughts, floods, and storms increase, climate change will drive population movements. The drivers of forced migration are climate processes and climate events. Climate processes are changes in sea level, desertification, water scarcity, and other conditions that occur slowly. Climate events are weather events and natural disasters—hurricanes, typhoons, flooding—that force populations to move immediately. Nonetheless, non-climate drivers such as poverty, population, and government policies also determine the vulnerability of communities to climate change, and some areas might become better places to live due to improved crop fertility or rainfall.

Put simply, climate change will cause population movements by making certain parts of the world much less viable places to live; by causing food and water supplies to become more unreliable and increasing the frequency and severity of floods and storms. Recent reports from the IPCC [Intergovernmental Panel on Climate Change] and elsewhere set out the parameters for what we can expect:

Oli Brown, *Migration and Climate Change*, IOM Migration Research Series, No. 31, 2008, pp. 16–20. Reproduced by permission.

By 2099 the world is expected to be on average between 1.8°C [3.2°F] and 4°C [7.2°F] hotter than it is now. Large areas are expected to become drier—the proportion of land in constant drought expected to increase from 2 per cent to 10 per cent by 2050. Meanwhile, the proportion of land suffering extreme drought is predicted to increase from 1 per cent at present to 30 per cent by the end of the 21st century. Rainfall patterns will change as the hydrological cycle becomes more intense. In some places this means that rain will be more likely to fall in deluges (washing away top-soil and causing flooding).

Changed rainfall patterns and a more intense hydrological cycle mean that extreme weather events such as droughts, storms and floods are expected to become increasingly frequent and severe. For example, it is estimated that the South Asian monsoon will become stronger with up to 20 per cent more rain falling on eastern India and Bangladesh by 2050. Conversely, less rain is expected at low to mid-latitudes; by 2050 sub-Saharan Africa is predicted to have up to 10 per cent less annual rainfall in its interior.

Less rain would have particularly serious impacts for sub-Saharan African agriculture which is largely rain-fed: the 2007 IPCC report of the Second Working Group estimates that yields from rain-fed agriculture could fall by up to 50 per cent by 2020. "Agricultural production, including access to food, in many African countries and regions is projected to be severely compromised by climate variability and change" the report notes.

According to the same report crop yields in central and south Asia could fall by 30 per cent by the middle of the 21st century. Some fish stocks will migrate towards the poles and colder waters and may deplete as surface water run-off and higher sea temperatures lead to more frequent hazardous algal blooms and coral bleaching. Compounding this, climate change is predicted to worsen a variety of health problems leading to more widespread malnutrition and diarrhoeal diseases, and altered distribution of some vectors of disease transmission such as the malarial mosquito.

Meanwhile, melting glaciers will increase the risk of flooding during the wet season and reduce dry-season water supplies to one-sixth of the world's population, predominantly in the Indian sub-continent, parts of China and the Andes. Melting glaciers will increase the risk of glacial lake outburst floods particularly in mountainous countries like Nepal, Peru and Bhutan.

Global average sea level, after accounting for coastal land uplift and subsidence, is projected to rise between 8 cm [3.1 in] and 13 cm [5.1 in] by 2030, between 17 cm [6.7 in] and 29 cm [11.4 in] by 2050, and between 35 cm and 82 cm by 2100 (depending on the model and scenario used). Large delta systems are at particular risk of flooding. The area of coastal wetlands is projected to decrease as a result of sea level rise. For a high emissions scenario and high climate sensitivity wetland loss could be as high as 25 per cent and 42 per cent of the world's existing coastal wetlands by the 2050s and 2100s respectively.

According to [researchers R. J.] Nicholls and [J.] Lowe, using a mid-range climate sensitivity projection, the number of people flooded per year is expected to increase by between 10 and 25 million per year by the 2050s and between 40 and 140 million per year by 2100s, depending on the future emissions scenario.

The avalanche of statistics above translates into a simple fact— that on current trends the "carrying capacity" of large parts of the world, i.e. the ability of different ecosystems to provide food, water and shelter for human populations, will be compromised by climate change.

Climate Processes and Climate Events

Robert McLeman of the University of Ottawa, unpacks the drivers of forced migration into two distinct groups. First, there are the climate drivers. These themselves are of two types—climate processes and climate events. *Climate processes* are slow-onset changes such as sea-level rise, salinization of agricultural land, desertification, growing water scarcity and food insecurity. Sea level rise patently makes certain coastal areas and small island states uninhabitable. Cumulatively they erode livelihoods and change the incentives to "stick it out" in a particular location. Some women in the Sahel, for example, already have to walk up to 25 kilometres [15.5 miles] a day to fetch water. If their journey gets longer they will simply have to move permanently.

On a national level sea level rise could have serious implications for food security and economic growth. This is a particular concern in countries that have a large part of their industrial capacity under the "one metre" zone. Bangladesh's Gangetic plain and the Nile Delta in Egypt, which are breadbaskets for both countries, are two such examples. Egypt's Nile Delta is one of the most densely populated areas of the world and is extremely vulnerable to sea level rise. A rise of just 1 metre would displace at least 6 million people and flood 4,500 km^2 [1737.5 mi^2] of farmland.

> *Cumulatively [climate processes] erode livelihoods and change the incentives to "stick it out" in a particular location.*

Climate events, on the other hand, are sudden and dramatic hazards such as monsoon floods, glacial lake outburst floods, storms, hurricanes and typhoons. These force people off their land much more quickly and dramatically. Hurricanes Katrina and Rita, for example, which lashed the Gulf Coast of the United States in August and September 2005 left an estimated 2 million people homeless. The *2000 World Disasters Report* estimated that 256 million people were affected by disasters (both weather-related and geo-physical) in the year 2000, up from an average of 211 million per year during the 1990s—an increase the Red Cross attributes to increased "hydro-meteorological" events.

Non-Climate Drivers

Equally important though are the non-climate drivers. It is clear that many natural disasters are, at least in part, "man-made". A natural hazard (such as an approaching storm) only becomes a "natural disaster" if a community is particularly *vulnerable* to its impacts. A tropical typhoon, for example, becomes a disaster if there is no early-warning system, the houses are poorly built and people are unaware of what to do in the event of a storm. A community's vulnerability, then, is a function of its *exposure* to climatic conditions (such as a coastal location) and the community's *adaptive capacity* (the capacity of a particular community to weather the worst of the storm and recover after it).

> *Climate change will challenge the adaptive capacities of many different communities, and overwhelm some, by interacting with and exacerbating existing problems of food security, water scarcity and the scant protection afforded by marginal lands.*

Different regions, countries and communities have very different adaptive capacities: pastoralist groups in the Sahel, for example, are socially, culturally and technically equipped to deal with a different range of natural hazards than, say, mountain dwellers in the Himalayas. National and individual wealth is one clear determinant of vulnerability—enabling better disaster risk reduction, disaster education and speedier responses. In the decade from 1994 to 2003 natural disasters in countries of high human development killed an average of 44 people per event, while disasters in countries of low human development killed an average of 300 people each.

On a national scale, Bangladesh has very different adaptive capacities and disaster resilience to the United States. In April 1991 Tropical Cyclone Gorky hit the Chittagong district of south-eastern Bangladesh. Winds of up to 260 kilometres [162 miles] per hour and a six-metre [19.7-foot] high storm surge battered much of the country killing at least 138,000 people and leaving as many as 10 million people homeless. The following year in August 1992, a *stronger* storm, the category five Hurricane Andrew, hit Florida and Louisiana with winds of 280 kilometres [174 miles] per hour and a 5.2-metre [17-foot] storm surge. But, while it left US$ 43 billion in damages in its wake, it caused only 65 deaths.

Climate change will challenge the adaptive capacities of many different communities, and overwhelm some, by interacting with and exacerbating existing problems of food security, water scarcity and the scant protection afforded by marginal lands. At some point that land becomes no longer capable of sustaining livelihoods and people will be forced to migrate to areas that present better opportunities. The "tipping points" will vary from place to place and from individual to individual. Natural disasters might displace large numbers of people for relatively short periods of time, but the slow-onset drivers are likely to displace permanently many more people in a less-headline grabbing way.

Population, Poverty, and Governance Are Key Variables

Migration, even forced migration, is not usually just a product of an environmental "push" from a *climate process* like sea level rise. Except in cases of *climate events*, where people flee for their lives, it does require some kind of "pull": be it environmental, social or economic. There has to be the hope of a better life elsewhere, however much of a gamble it might be. Past environmental migratory movements, such as in the US Dust Bowl years in the 1930s, suggest that being able to migrate away from severe climatic conditions, in this case prolonged drought, requires would-be migrants to have some "social and financial capital" such as existing support networks in the destination area and the funds to be able to move.

It also should be mentioned, and this is absent from much of the campaigning literature, that climate change will make some places *better able* to sustain larger populations. This is particularly reflected in predictions for less-severe total temperature rises, i.e. 2 to 3°C [3.6 to 5.4°F] over the 21st century rather than rise of 4 to 5 degrees [7.2 to 9°F] or more. This is for three main reasons. First, higher temperatures will likely extend growing seasons and reduce frost risk in mid to high-latitude areas such as Europe, Australia and New Zealand and make new crops viable (already vineyards are spreading north in Britain). Second, the "fertilization effect" of more CO_2 in the atmosphere is predicted to increase crop yields and the density of vegetation in some areas. And third, altered rainfall patterns mean that rain might increase in areas previously suffering water stress. A 2005 study, for example, predicts that a warmer north Atlantic and hotter Sahara will trigger more rain for the Sahel. It is not inconceivable then that there might be migration in order to take advantage of the effects of climate change.

In other words, climate change might provide both "push" and "pull" for some population displacement. This is not to downplay the seriousness of climate change: above 4 or 5°C [7.2 or 9°F] the predicted impacts of climate change become almost universally negative. But it is to make that point that the role of climate change in population displacement is not a linear relationship of cause and effect, of environmental "push" and economic "pull".

Non-climatic drivers remain a key variable. It is, after all, population growth, income distribution and government policy that push people to live on marginal lands in the first place. In other words a community's vulnerability to climate change is not a constant—it can be increased or decreased for reasons that have nothing to do with greenhouse gas emissions. In this sense it is the non-climatic drivers (that put vulnerable people in marginal situations) that can be as important a determinant of the problem as the strength of the "climate signal" itself.

[T]he role of climate change in population displacement is not a linear relationship of cause and effect, of environmental "push" and economic "pull".

As Steve Lonergan of the University of Victoria, Canada, noted in 1998, "there is too often an uncritical acceptance of a direct causal link between environmental degradation and population displacement. Implicit in these writings is the belief that environmental degradation—as a possible cause of population displacement—can be separated from other social, economic or political causes. It must be recognized that the degradation of the environment is socially and spatially constructed; only through a structural understanding of the environment in the broader political and cultural context of a region or country can one begin to understand the "role" it plays as a factor in population movement".

Intuitively we can see how climate change might play a role in future movements of people. But putting empirically sound figures on the extent of the problem is complex. And it is hard to persuade decision makers to take the issue seriously without being able to wave concrete figures in front of them. . . .

4

Climate Change Will Force the Relocation of Animal Species

Mary-Lou Considine

Mary-Lou Considine is editor of ECOS, a bimonthly magazine that reports on sustainability with a scientific perspective.

Some scientists recommend the relocation of select species threatened by climate change to increase their chances of survival in the wild. Increasingly rapid changes in the environment caused by man-made global warming outpace the abilities of many species to adapt. In order for this approach to be successful, it is advised that relocation be pursued as a last resort—after efforts to preserve a species in its natural habitat—and not before the risks are properly assessed or after the population dips to dangerously low numbers. In particular cases, the survival of a species hinges directly on climate change, and relocation is required immediately.

Time is fast running out for one of Australia's most charismatic marsupials, the threatened mountain pygmy possum (*Burramys parvus*). This delicate animal is only found within a 3-4 sq km [1.1-1.5 sq mi] area of the Australian Alps where it hibernates in winter under snow. Modest though its habitat may be, the species' range is set to shrink rapidly this century if global warming continues at its current rate.

Mary-Lou Considine, "Moving On: Relocating Species in Response to Climate Change," *ECOS*, May 4, 2011. http://www.ecosmagazine.com and http://www.publish.csiro.au. Copyright © 2012 by the 522846 Commonwealth Scientific and Industrial Research Organization CSIRO PUBLISHING. All rights reserved. Reproduced by permission.

How can we help this animal adapt to a changing climate and habitat? If snow cover all but disappears, there will be no opportunity to create a protected habitat corridor—an 'emergency exit'—for *B. parvus* to retreat to.

Its best chance of surviving in the wild, say some scientists, is to move small populations to a new 'home' in forested areas below the snow-line—outside the species' current range. The basis of this proposal is evidence from the fossil record showing *B. parvus* was once widespread at lower altitudes.

'Option of Last Resort'

Moving species for conservation purposes is not new. More than 200 translocations and reintroductions of 42 vertebrate species have been carried out in Australia since European settlement.

However, all relocations to date have been carried out in response to tangible threats such as introduced pests or diseases, stock grazing, land clearing or hydroelectricity works. Under current environmental regulation—particularly the federal *Environmental Protection and Biodiversity Conservation (EPBC) Act 1999*—there is no provision for relocating species in response to climate change.

Yet scientists point out that the unprecedented speed of anthropogenic climate change will outpace the adaptive capacity of many species. Rapid climate change has already caused changes to distribution of many plants and animals, leading in some cases to extinctions. And scientists predict entire ecosystems such as cloud forests and coral reefs could disappear by the end of the century.

Late last year [in 2010], the Terrestrial Biodiversity Adaptation Research Network, funded through the National Climate Change Adaptation Research Facility (NCCARF), ran a workshop at which ecologists and policy makers debated the environmental, ethical and policy aspects of managed relocation. Workshop participants concluded that managed relocation 'is not a panacea to climate change adaptation for biodiversity and is pointless without a substantial commitment to mitigation, ongoing management of existing threats and a belief in the community that biodiversity can and should be conserved'.

Macquarie University's Professor Lesley Hughes—a Commissioner with the recently established Climate Commission, and a co-convenor of the Terrestrial Biodiversity Adaptation Research Network—agrees the approach should be seen as an 'option of last resort'.

In an earlier collaboration, Prof Hughes was involved in developing a broad risk assessment framework for policy makers and conservation agencies that begins with more conventional options for conserving species. This emphasis on conservation *in situ* acknowledges the risk of managed relocation becoming a 'distraction' from climate change mitigation and habitat protection efforts.

Using the framework, managers would first evaluate opportunities for reducing the level of non-climate impacts—such as pests, weeds, frequent fire or habitat degradation—on the species. 'We simply need to do a lot better at managing existing, long-term threats,' says Prof Hughes.

The next step would be to assess the potential for species to move 'under their own steam' into new climate zones via habitat corridors carved out of the landscape.

'That's not going to fix everything because most species don't move far enough each year to keep up with the rate of climate change,' explains Prof Hughes. 'For some species there may be other things you could do *in situ*. For example, if nesting sites are a limiting factor, you could provide artificial nests to build up a population.'

Managed relocation is a last resort. 'There'll be a subset of species that we will simply watch decline and become extinct, unless we take concrete action,' says Prof Hughes. 'That's when we have to acknowledge that, while there are risks involved in moving them, the risk of leaving them where they are is greater.'

[M]ost species don't move far enough each year to keep up with the rate of climate change.

One of the most serious risks associated with managed relocation is the potential to create new pest problems at the target site.

The more detailed knowledge scientists have about a species *in situ* and in the new habitat, the more robust will be the models they develop for managers. Prof Hughes' team has already begun experimenting with moving plants to warmer areas to identify possible future responses of insect communities in the receiving habitats.

The Right Moment

Timing is critical to the success of managed relocation. Move it too soon and precious conservation resources might be wasted on a species that could have adapted to climate change *in situ*, says Dr Tara Martin of CSIRO's [The Commonwealth Scientific and Industrial Research Organisation] Ecosystem Sciences. But delaying relocation until species' numbers have dropped to dangerously low levels and genetic diversity is eroded will impede the chances of a successful move.

'A lot of discussion around managed relocation has been about the risk of the species in a new area becoming invasive, or the risk of the species becoming extinct if you do nothing,' says Dr Martin.

'We are trying to provide a modelling framework for moving beyond that. If you do decide to undertake managed relocation, when would you do it? If you move a species too early without knowing enough about the impact of climate change and the potential risks of the species to the new habitat, we may end up wasting resources and the species becoming problematic.

'On the other hand, if you wait and collect more data, you may learn more about the impact of climate change on the species, but by the time you have a good understanding of the impacts, you may have missed the boat.' . . .

The CSIRO framework enables managers to determine when to carry out the move, weighing the biological and socioeconomic costs of relocation, species' risk of extinction, and risk to the receiving site against predicted benefits.

"The most suitable scenario is when the risk of extinction of the target species is high but the risk to the existing ecosystem at the receiving site is low."

'While managed relocation will be used in some specific circumstances for species that we really value, it will not be a saviour for all biodiversity in the face of climate change,' adds Dr Martin.

'The most suitable scenario is when the risk of extinction of the target species is high but the risk to the existing ecosystem at the receiving site is low.'

A Case for Immediate Action?

Since 1970, south-west Western Australia—a globally recognised biodiversity hotspot—has become drier as average annual rainfall has dropped.

This drier climate is posing a major threat to the western swamp tortoise (*Pseudemydura umbrina*). Two wild populations of less than 100 survive in adjacent reserves near Perth—the smallest wild populations of any Australian reptile. Two other populations have been established with translocated individuals from a captive breeding program at Perth Zoo.

Associate Professor Nicki Mitchell of the University of Western Australia and PhD student, Sophie Arnall, are working with the WA Department of Environment and Conservation (DECWA) and Perth Zoo to develop models for identifying viable habitat alternatives for the species—with the key element being pooled water. Unlike other tortoises, the western swamp tortoise feeds and breeds in shallow swamps in winter and aestivates (sleeps) in summer.

'These tortoises are active when the swamps are meant to [be] full,' says Assoc Prof Mitchell. 'The swamps used to hold water for 6 to 7 months in the 1960s, but 3 to 4 months is more typical.

'This means females aren't reproducing so often because they're not getting as much energy to allocate to eggs. It also means the hatchlings that emerge the following year have a very short growing season. They need to be a decent size before they first aestivate, otherwise they desiccate.

'The models will help us identify where to put these animals to give them the best chance of surviving. We think south is the way to go because that's where the rainfall will provide better hydrological conditions.'

While Assoc Prof Mitchell believes managed relocation may be some way off for many species, she feels the situation of the western swamp tortoise—a species whose survival is directly linked to climate change—presents a clear-cut case for action.

'These animals don't breed quickly. They live for up to 70 years, don't breed until they're 10–15, and produce only 3–5 eggs. They're not going to run amok like cane toads, and they've already been released in novel sites where they have had no adverse impacts.

'This species is the only survivor of an ancient linage of Australian tortoises, and you would argue it would be nice to maintain them in the wild for future generations.'

5

Climate Change Adaptation Is More Important than Mitigation

Marco Visscher

Marco Visscher is editor-at-large for news magazine Ode *and a journalist based in Rotterdam, The Netherlands.*

Mitigating climate change will require a radical transformation in the way people live and how energy is produced and consumed. Carbon emissions policies must also be put into place in order to significantly affect the global economy and call for historic political agreements. Hence, a focus on adaptation has gained support as a more practical and creative approach. It would allow geographically diverse communities to prepare for the varying impacts of global warming and is effective regardless of its causes or success in cutting emissions. Also, adaptation is more realistic than mitigation for developing countries, which face more immediate threats such as poverty and are more vulnerable to disasters related to climate change.

It probably won't make you any friends if you say it out loud, but preventing further global warming is going to be a pain in the neck.

To combat climate change, we have to emit fewer greenhouse gases. The way we consume and produce energy will have to change radically. Our lifestyles will have to be revised so drastically that even diehard anti-materialists will protest.

Marco Visscher, "A Politically Incorrect Solution to Climate Change," *Ode*, June 2011. Reproduced by permission.

The solution requires the adoption of a massive CO_2 tax, which will substantially affect the world economy, with unknown consequences. It requires every country—rich and poor—to cooperate on political protocols.

No wonder the process has been such an uphill battle.

A More Affordable, Practical and Effective Approach

But a different perspective is emerging, an approach that seems far more affordable, practical and effective—adaptation. Adaptation refers to the ability to develop creative strategies that reduce our vulnerability to the effects of climate change, such as building better flood defenses, constructing irrigation systems and installing hurricane strapping to prevent roofs from blowing away during hurricanes and heavy storms.

Adaptation won't slow the warming of the Earth's surface, but it will give communities the resilience to absorb its damaging effects. And that's at least as essential. Climate change may be a global phenomenon, but its impact on regions varies widely. "Adaptation enables us to intelligently tailor our response," writes former British politician Nigel Lawson in *An Appeal to Reason: A Cool Look at Global Warming*, his critical analysis of the science of climate change.

Critics contend that adapting our societies to the effects of global warming is not enough. According to Joe Romm, an influential climate change blogger, we will experience so many extreme weather events that our capacity to adapt will be overwhelmed. "I think the term 'adaptation' doesn't make it clear enough that it's going to be very hard," says Romm. "I fear that what people describe as 'adaptation' is going to be a lot of suffering."

Others believe that even the suggestion of accepting that the Earth is warming will irrevocably damage our ability to combat climate change by mitigation, or reducing greenhouse gas emissions. As a result, adaptation has long been a politically incorrect idea. Former U.S. Vice-President Al Gore accurately described the sentiment in his 1992 book *Earth in the Balance*: "Believing that we can adapt to just about anything is ultimately a kind of laziness, an arrogant faith in our ability to react in time to save our skin."

Of course, the two strategies—adaptation and mitigation—can peacefully co-exist. Roger Pielke, Jr., author of *The Climate Fix: What Scientists and Politicians Won't Tell You About Global-Warming*, thinks it's unfortunate that they are often portrayed as opposites. "No matter what part of natural threats are due to climate change, it still makes sense to build better dikes and have evacuation plans," he says. "Adaptation and mitigation address different issues on different time scales with different effects."

Can a change of focus from mitigation to adaptation breathe new life into a dead-end conversation that threatens to lose the public's interest?

And yet, with a little goodwill, the agreement world leaders reached in Copenhagen in 2009 can be called a breakthrough. It mentions the word "adaptation" no less than 11 times, just one fewer than "mitigation," which has been pursued—with little success—since the historic 1992 climate change convention adopted during the UN's [United Nations] Earth Summit in Rio de Janeiro. And though it is still unclear how to raise and distribute the funds necessary to help countries adapt to a warmer world, experts say this hurdle will be much easier to jump. Can a change of focus from mitigation to adaptation breathe new life into a dead-end conversation that threatens to lose the public's interest?

The realization that living creatures are capable of adapting to a changing environment is hardly revolutionary. Over the millennia, humanity has become quite proficient at it. People are constantly devising creative solutions. They develop innovative technology; they subdue natural threats; they adjust to the change; they move away. Temperature variations are not new, either. Humanity has survived earlier eras that were colder or warmer than today and with vastly fewer financial and technological means, let alone scientific predictions on the changes to come.

Humanity is far from alone in its ability to adapt. In a warmer world, birds fly higher where the air is cooler, or they move to more suitable areas. Squirrels in northern Canada's Yukon have adapted to spring's earlier arrival by giving birth 18 days sooner than their great-grandparents did, enabling them to profit from the pine cones that appear earlier in the year. Because Europe's warmer spring makes caterpillars turn into butterflies sooner, titmice lay their eggs sooner so the chicks can still eat the caterpillars. A recent study from the University of British Columbia demonstrated that sticklebacks can easily tolerate a change in temperature of 4.5 degrees Fahrenheit (2.5 degrees Celsius) over a three-year period.

A Blind Focus on Reducing Emissions

The problem, of course, is the warming predicted for the coming century. The central conclusion drawn by the IPCC [Intergovernmental Panel on Climate Change], the UN's climate panel, is well known: The Earth is gradually warming, primarily as a result of greenhouse gases. By the year 2100, our nearest estimates predict that the average temperature of the Earth's surface will rise 3.2 degrees Fahrenheit (1.8 degrees Celsius) in the best-case scenario and 7.2 degrees Fahrenheit (4 degrees Celsius) in the worst case. Making predictions further into the future is nearly impossible. These reports, which reflect current thinking in climate science, are filled with implications for all kinds of environments, in all kinds of scenarios. But the recommended policy is unambiguous: Reduce greenhouse gas emissions.

Nonetheless, the doubters and skeptics abound. They contend that a blind focus on reducing greenhouse gas emissions silences every other potential explanation for global warming. Even if climate activists were to see their dreams of a historic agreement become reality, the Earth might continue to heat up as a result of other causes, the research into which enjoys far less support. Increased solar activity could influence the Earth's temperature or the impact of atmospheric water vapor and clouds might partially explain global warming, to name just two theories that have been summarily rejected.

That's why skeptics believe adaptation is more effective. It helps, regardless of the exact cause of climate change, regardless of the success (or failure) of climate negotiations. And some think the modern obsession with greenhouse gases hampers our ability to meet the challenge of arming ourselves against disaster, especially in poor countries.

"With adaptation you can pocket the benefits of the effects of global warming . . . and reduce the harm caused by it."

Moreover—prepare for yet another politically incorrect idea—higher temperatures have advantages, skeptics claim. They point out, for example, that the IPCC predicts food production will increase this century as a result of improved agricultural conditions and that extreme cold always claims more victims than extreme heat. And wouldn't you know, temperatures are predicted to rise most in the planet's coldest regions. "With adaptation you can pocket the benefits of the effects of global warming," says Lawson, "and reduce the harm caused by it."

Lawson is extremely critical of the climate change debate. "People think that if the problem is caused by man-made carbon dioxide emissions, then the solution must be to reduce them," he says. "That's a fallacy. You must do what's cost-effective and what's politically realistic." Others, however, claim that letting nature take its course is too expensive, and the fact that reducing CO_2 will be difficult does not mean we shouldn't try.

Cities Ideally Equipped to Prepare

What does adaptation look like? If any country can answer that question, it's the Netherlands. More than 1,000 years ago, Dutch farmers were digging ditches to make the sodden ground arable. The Dutch have successfully tamed the water. The Netherlands is rich in rivers, and more than half its land lies below sea level, yet the country does not live in fear of rapidly rising seas and increased precipitation. Adaptation is a theme familiar to the Dutch.

"If the Netherlands had not learned to adapt to an ever-changing environment, it would have been lost to the sea long ago," said, former Dutch Prime Minister Jan Peter Balkenende when he chaired a 2007 UN climate event session. Balkenende, who lost family members to a 1953 storm that breached the country's southwestern dikes, proudly described the Delta Works, a complex project built in the Netherlands in 1986 and consisting of reinforced dikes and dunes, closed-off sea inlets and storm surge barriers.

Now, the Netherlands is anticipating the variables inherent in climate change. Engineers are investigating the value of raising dikes and widening rivers. Project developers are building neighborhoods filled with floating homes. Planners are designating areas that can be temporarily submerged when rivers overflow. Urban developers are considering residential areas built on raised embankments. Architects are placing meters for water and electricity in attics rather than on ground floors. On the international development front, the Netherlands is working with Indonesia to reclaim land near Semarang, a city on the island of Java with more than a million inhabitants, to protect the city center from flooding.

Cities are ideally equipped to prepare for climate change, says Matthew Kahn, a professor of environmental economics at UCLA and author of *Climatopolis: How Our Cities Will Thrive in the Hotter Future.* "In cities, people live and work inside, relative to farmers in rural areas, so urbanites can protect themselves and their buildings with ventilation and insulation," Kahn writes. "When we build houses, bridges and cities, we can take expectations of a changing climate into account." He cites the floating homes architect Thom Mayne developed for New Orleans residents after Hurricane Katrina destroyed their city as a case in point. Kahn, whose book is reviled by climate activists, has complete faith in the free market. "If you have 7 billion people worried about climate change, that's a major economic opportunity," he explains. According to Kahn, entrepreneurs will recognize the market potential of innovations that allow us to soften the effects of global warming, from energy-efficient air conditioners to flood-proof homes. "Historically, cities are centers of innovation, where people have always come up with new ideas to cope with a changing world—and now, a changing climate."

But Romm wonders if that optimism is realistic. "People knew New Orleans would be flooded one day, yet nobody built levees," he counters. "And now ... years after [Hurricane] Katrina, it still doesn't have enough protection against a similar disaster."

Mitigation Harder on Developing Nations

A common argument advanced by proponents of adaptation is that the alternative, mitigation, is much harder on developing nations. Emerging economies such as China, India and Brazil have made it clear that they are not interested in tempering their explosive growth by lowering greenhouse gas emissions. Poor countries are equally uninterested and have subtly noted that they are not the source of the problem in any case, an understandable viewpoint. Poor countries hope to become more affluent as quickly as possible before reserving money to solve a problem slated for the future. In Lawson's words, "It's immoral to ask the people in developing countries to cut back on their carbon emissions when they are dealing with poverty and disease."

Poor countries are more vulnerable than rich countries to the expected increase in flooding, droughts, hurricanes and heat waves. This isn't because they'll be confronted with more natural disasters, but because economic development provides insurance against a disaster's aftershocks; those who have things of value ensure they're protected.

Poor countries are equally uninterested and have subtly noted that they are not the source of the problem in any case, an understandable viewpoint.

That also explains why the earthquake in Haiti claimed so many more lives than the considerably harsher earthquake in Chile six weeks later. In the UN's Human Development Index, which weighs factors such as the size of a country's economy and its citizens' average life expectancy, Haiti is near the bottom at No. 149 while Chile comes in at a respectable 44, between Hungary and Croatia.

To Indur Goklany, a science and technology policy analyst for the U.S. Department of the Interior, the situation is clear. "In developing countries, the adaptational capacity is currently low. And so we need more economic development. If these countries had more economic progress, they would be better capable of adapting."

Interestingly enough, economic growth is precisely what experts—including those at the IPCC—predict for a warmer world. And that growth is expected to be spectacular. Even in the most somber scenario—in which the IPCC assumes runaway population growth, minimal technological advancement and the lowest standard of living—rich countries would grow

1 percent every year; poor countries would grow 2.3 percent. At the end of the century, our great-grandchildren in rich countries would be two-and-a-half times wealthier than we are today; in poor countries, the figure would be a stunning nine times wealthier.

Amid the warnings that future generations will be worse off and we must invest heavily to avert doom, this math supports adaptation advocates. "I can't see the logic in putting aside money for decades without any obvious benefit," Goklany says. "Developing countries have many immediate threats, but global warming isn't one of them."

This optimism about the opportunities the future holds is seldom shared by climate activists. Romm puts it this way: "People are kidding themselves if they think we're going to be so rich that we can buy our way out of devastation." Critics claim that economic growth will slow down, not speed up, as a result of climate change, and a reliance on adaptation, they argue, could mean that investments in clean technologies, for example, will be neglected. A change of focus from mitigation to adaptation can be viewed as a pragmatic escape from political deadlock, but that doesn't mean it will happen. It's also possible, perhaps even likely, that environmental groups' vested interests and politicians' maneuvering will prolong the search for a way to prevent climate change. Whatever you think about mitigation versus adaptation, delay is certainly something we cannot afford.

6

Climate Change Mitigation Is More Important than Adaptation

Joe Romm

Joe Romm is a senior fellow at the Center for American progress, a progressive think tank, and author of Hell and High Water: Global Warming—the Solution and the Politics—and What We Should Do.

If the concentration of carbon dioxide in the atmosphere is not aggressively maintained, the world faces disastrous consequences; the sea level will rise six inches a decade, one-third of the earth will become desert, and more than 70 percent of all species will go extinct. Clearly, an emphasis on adaptation—not mitigation—in response to climate change is a backward approach. Technological breakthroughs, for instance, are heralded to replace fossil-based fuels and energy, but they are rare and can take decades to achieve significant impacts. Adaptation advocates also confuse their efforts with mitigation, undermining their own arguments. To minimize human suffering, a decisive focus must be placed on stopping climate change.

The wheels may be falling off the media's climate discussion, if a new *L.A. Times* piece is any evidence. The piece, "Global warming: Just deal with it, some scientists say," which is really an article about not dealing with it.

The *L.A. Times*, with the help of the delayer-1000 du jour [environmental studies professor], Roger Pielke. Jr., has brought to prominence (and fallen for) what I call the "adaptation trap":

> The adaptation trap is the belief that 1) "it would be easier and cheaper to adapt than fight climate change" [as the *Times* puts it in the sub-head] and/or 2) "adaptation" to climate change is possible in any meaningful sense of the word absent an intense mitigation effort starting now to keep carbon dioxide concentrations below 450 ppm [parts per million].

Sorry for the long definition, but as we'll see, the second part is especially critical in what has now become an important emerging policy debate, which is cleverly devoid of specifics. (Indeed, on his blog, Pielke says he was misquoted and denies he believes the first part, which actually makes the *L.A.T.* piece even lamer, as Grist's Dave Roberts shows). And being misquoted doesn't mean Pielke isn't very wrong anyway—as we'll see at the end, Pielke is so confused about adaptation and mitigation that he takes the prize for the most backward analogy in the history of the climate debate and unintentionally proves just how wrong he is.

You see, as I've been arguing, the real question for the world is not whether we can stabilize below 450 ppm of atmospheric carbon dioxide if we try hard enough and fast enough—of course we can, and at a very low cost according to the Intergovernmental Panel on Climate Change, which self-described "nonskeptical heretics" like Pielke claim to believe in.

The real question for humanity is whether we can avoid 800 to 1000 ppm or more. That is what the delayers and nonskeptical heretics simply don't understand. At 800 to 1000 ppm, the world faces multiple catastrophes, including:

1. Sea level rise of 80 feet to 250 feet at a rate of 6 inches a decade (or more).

2. Desertification of one third the planet and drought over half the planet, plus the loss of all inland glaciers.

3. More than 70% of all species going extinct, plus extreme ocean acidification. . . .

This Hell and High Water could be "adapted" to by billions and billions of people only in the sense that the citizens of New Orleans "adapted" to Hurricane Katrina or that people in Darfur have "adapted" to their military conflict. Such "adaptation" is better called "suffering" as former AAAS [the American Association for the Advancement of Science] President John Holdren describes it in talks.

What will it take to avoid 800 to 1000 ppm? Remember the IPCC bombshell from last year:

Based on current understanding of climate carbon cycle feedback . . . to stabilise at 1000 ppm this feedback could require that cumulative emissions be reduced from a model average of approximately 1415 [1340 to 1490] GtC [gigatons of carbon] to approximately 1100 [980 to 1250] GtC.

This Hell and High Water could be "adapted" to by billions and billions of people only in the sense that the citizens of New Orleans "adapted" to Hurricane Katrina . . .

That means that to have confidence of avoiding 1000 ppm, we need to have average annual carbon emission substantially below 11 billion tons a year, or average annual carbon dioxide emissions much below 40 billion tons a year. Note: We're at about 30 billion tons of C02 annually and rising more than 3% a year. We'll probably be over 40 billion by 2020. Just staying at the 2020 level for another 8 decades would require immediate action and strong national and global measures for a century.

That of course is why I try not to waste a lot of time debating skeptics/doubters/deniers/delayers/"heretics"/climate-destroyers until and unless they answer the question:

> "If you were running national and global climate policy, what level of global CO_2 concentrations would be your goal and how would you achieve it?"

If you can't or won't answer that, then in my blog you're a "Delayer-1000" meaning it is time to start recounting the likely impacts of 1000 ppm and move on because such a person is not a serious contributor to the climate debate.

I posed the question to Pielke on this blog over a week ago—but he offered no reply. I have gone through the past few months of his posts—oh, the things I do for this blog [*don't worry, readers, I had plenty of coffee on hand*]—and can't actually find out what specifically he would do, which is typical of delayers.

The Technology Trap

He does endorse analysis by [environmental economics expert] Chris Green, who thinks emissions targets are the *problem* and that cutting CO_2 emissions in half by 2050 [which is needed to stabilize at or below 450 ppm] is "for all intents and purposes out of the question" because "the replacement of fossil-based energy systems by carbon-emission-free system to any significant degree awaits science and engineering-based technological breakthroughs."

Yes, it's the old "technological breakthroughs" canard, or as I call it, the "technology trap"—the first and last refuge of those who either don't really want to take action or who understand less about energy technology than they do about the climate. To repeat an as-yet undebunked point I've made many times (most notably here but also in talks to some of the leading energy experts in the world)—in the energy arena:

- Technological breakthroughs hardly ever happen.

- Even when they do happen, they rarely have a transformative impact on energy markets, even over a span of decades.

If we had to wait for multiple science and engineering-based technological breakthroughs to stabilize below 450 ppm (or even below 800 ppm), then we could write the obituary for a livable climate right now. But we don't. I (and others) have laid out the key solutions many times in this blog (and at length in my book), and I will detail more of them this year. But I digress.

No surprise that Pielke has become a fellow at the Breakthrough Institute—yes this is [Michael] Shellenberger's and [Ted] Nordhaus's think tank, which should tell you all you need to know. ... That said, S&N support [President Barack] Obama's terrific climate plan, so I'd be quite interested to know if Pielke does too, because if so, he isn't a Delayer-1000 (but then again, he wouldn't be a "heretic" either).

Pielke's use of the term "nonskeptical heretic," which he coined, is of course a clever and wholly unjustified attack on real climate scientists. After all, "Heresy is a challenge to a prescribed system of belief, especially a religious one." The firm belief in the urgent need for action is not a religious belief. It is a rational response to our scientific understanding of the problem, as I've explained, which is based on a well-tested theory and many real-world observations—the oppositive of religion.

Pielke isn't a heretic of anything. He is a delayer, maybe a delayer-1000.

One thing is for certain, Pielke is very, very confused about adaptation and mitigation. He calls for "rejecting bad policy arguments when offered in the way of substitutes for adaptation, like the tired old view that today's disaster losses are somehow a justification for changes to energy policies." This tired old straw man is not a primary justification for changes to energy policy made by any climate or energy expert I know. Hurricanes and major droughts are used to to indicate the impact of permanent changes like sea level rise and desertification—I make that argument all the time.

The question is whether we are going to have lots of (avoidable) suffering too, because we failed to do enough mitigation fast enough.

The Most Backward Analogy You've Ever Seen

Lots of adaptation is inevitable, in part thanks to the success of the deniers and delayers. The question is whether we are going to have lots of (avoidable) suffering too, because we failed to do enough mitigation fast enough. And this brings us to one of the biggest howlers I've ever seen in the entire climate debate, from Pielke's recent post:

> If mitigation advocates do not like being told that their misleading arguments poorly serve policy debate, well, they should probably try to come up with a more robust set of arguments. Arguing that support for adaptation undercuts support for mitigation is a little like making the argument that support for *eating healthy and getting exercise (adapting one's lifestyle)* undercuts support for heart surgery research (mitigating the effects of heart disease). Obviously we should seek both adaptation and mitigation in the context of heart disease.

No, no, no, no. No wonder Pielke is so confused. He labels adaptation what is in fact mitigation, and his idea of mitigation is apparently research into adaptation. This must be the most backward analogy I've ever seen. He actually makes the best case against himself.

"Eating healthy and getting exercise" are not "adapting one's lifestyle"—they are changing one's actions substantially to prevent heart disease in the first place. That is prevention. That is mitigation. Switching your diet is analogous to switching to low-carbon fuels. And if eating healthy means eating less, or eating less of bad foods, that would be energy efficiency. Exercise may be closer analogy to driving your car less and riding a bike instead.

Heart surgery is adaptation—it's waiting until the bad outcome has occurred (heart disease) and then trying desperately to save yourself with no guarantee of success. Lots of people die on the operating table or later from complications. Pielke apparently thinks the best that mitigators can do for people at risk of heart disease is research into methods of better surgery for dealing with it.

The correct analogy is that mitigators want to prevent heart disease in the first place, with things like diet and exercise, since adapting to heart disease may turn out to be impossible for many people, no matter how great our surgical/medical means of adapting is. Some people with heart disease will have to restrict their activity, others will have a shorter life or be in constant pain, and others will simply die of a heart attack or complications from surgery.

Such adaptation is a gamble with possibly catastrophic outcomes—whereas smart mitigation can with high confidence dramatically decrease one's chances of bad outcomes (like heart attacks and death) and dramatically increase one's chances of good outcomes (a long healthy life). Sound analogous to our current dilemma? So let's focus the vast majority of our effort on immediate and strong climate mitigation to minimize suffering, and do what adaptation we are forced to by our unconscionable delay.

7

Climate Change Must Be Addressed in Developing Countries

Economist

The Economist *is a weekly news and international affairs publication based in London, the United Kingdom.*

The contribution of the developing world to climate change is underestimated; low- and middle-income nations currently produce more than half of all carbon emissions. Their vulnerabilities to global warming are even greater. The costs to gross domestic product and devastation caused by rising temperatures are disproportionate in poor countries, which suffer from inadequate housing, poorer health, and insufficient medical care. Water supplies, crop yields, and disease also are indirectly impacted in these regions. While things are at equal stake for them as rich countries in reaching a climate-change deal, poor countries face obstacles in the sheer costs of mitigation, views on emissions responsibility, and ineffective public administration.

In late April [2009] Mostafa Rokonuzzaman, a farmer in south-western Bangladesh, gave an impassioned speech at a public meeting in his village, complaining that climate change, freakish hot spells and failed rains were ruining his vegetables. He didn't know the half of it. A month later Mr Rokonuzzaman was chest-deep in a flood that had swept away his house, farm and even the village where the meeting took place. Cyclone Aila (its effects pictured above) which caused the storm surge that breached the village's flood barriers, was itself a plausible example of how climate change is wreaking devastation in poor countries.

The Scale of Climate Change for Poor Countries

Most people in the West know that the poor world contributes to climate change, though the scale of its contribution still comes as a surprise. Poor and middle-income countries already account for just over half of total carbon emissions; Brazil produces more CO_2 per head than Germany. The lifetime emissions from these countries' planned power stations would match the world's entire industrial pollution since 1850.

Less often realised, though, is that global warming does far more damage to poor countries than they do to the climate. In a report in 2006 Nicholas (now Lord) Stern calculated that a 2°C [3.6°F] rise in global temperature cost about 1% of world GDP [gross domestic product]. But the World Bank, in its new [2010] World Development Report, now says the cost to Africa will be more like 4% of GDP and to India, 5%. Even if environmental costs were distributed equally to every person on earth, developing countries would still bear 80% of the burden (because they account for 80% of world population). As it is, they bear an even greater share, though their citizens' carbon footprints are much smaller.

As December [2009]'s Copenhagen summit on climate change draws near, poor countries are expressing alarm at the slow pace of negotiations to replace the Kyoto protocol. Agreed (partially) in 1997, this bound rich countries to cut their greenhouse-gas emissions by 5.2% from 1990 levels by 2012.

Counting the cost of global warming is hard because no one really knows how much to attribute to climate change and how much to other factors. But one indication of its rising costs is the number of people around the world affected by natural disasters. In 1981–85, fewer than 500m people required international disaster-assistance; in 2001–05, the number reached 1.5 billion. This includes 4% of the population of the poorest countries and over 7% in lower-middle-income countries.

In all, reckons the World Health Organisation, climate change caused a loss of 5.5m disability-adjusted life years (a measure of harm to human health) in 2000, most of it in Africa and Asia. Estimates by the Global Humanitarian Forum, a Swiss think-tank, and in a study in *Comparative Quantification of Health Risks*, a scientific journal, put the number of additional deaths attributable to climate change every year at 150,000. The indirect harm, through its impact on water supplies, crop yields and disease is hugely greater.

More Vulnerable than the Rich

The poor are more vulnerable than the rich for several reasons. Flimsy housing, poor health and inadequate health care mean that natural disasters of all kinds hurt them more. When Hurricane Mitch swept through Honduras in 1998, for example, poor households lost 15–20% of their assets but the rich lost only 3%.

Global warming aggravates that. It also increases the chances of catching the life-threatening diseases that are more prevalent in poorer countries. In many places cities have been built just above a so-called "malaria line", above which malaria-bearing mosquitoes cannot survive (Nairobi is one example). Warmer weather allows the bugs to move into previously unaffected altitudes, spreading a disease that is already the biggest killer in Africa. By 2030 climate change may expose 90m more people to malaria in Africa alone. Similarly, meningitis outbreaks in Africa are strongly correlated with drought. Both are likely to increase. Diarrhoea is forecast to rise 5% by 2020 in poor countries because of climate change. Dengue fever has been expanding its range: its incidence doubled in parts of the Americas between 1995–97 and 2005–07. On one estimate, 60% of the world's population will be exposed to the disease by 2070.

Next, as Mr Rokonuzzaman's story showed, poor countries are particularly prone to flooding. Ten of the developing world's 15 largest cities are in low-lying coastal areas vulnerable to rising sea levels or coastal surges. They include Shanghai, Mumbai and Cairo. In South and East Asia the floodplains of great rivers have always been home to vast numbers of people and much economic activity. Climate change is overwhelming the social and other arrangements that in the past allowed countries and people to cope with floods. National budgets can ill afford the cost of improving defences. The Netherlands is also affected and is spending $100 per person a year on flood defences. In Bangladesh that sum is a quarter of the average person's annual income.

By 2030 climate change may expose 90m more people to malaria in Africa alone.

Gravely Affecting Main Economic Activities

The biggest vulnerability is that the weather gravely affects developing countries' main economic activities—such as farming and tourism. Global warming dries out farmland. Since two-thirds of Africa is desert or arid, the continent is heavily exposed. One study predicts that by 2080 as much as a fifth of Africa's farmland will be severely stressed. And that is only one part of the problem.

Global warming also seems to be speeding up the earth's hydrologic cycle, causing both floods and droughts (more rains fall in shorter periods, with longer gaps between). In addition, by melting glaciers, global warming reduces nature's storage capacity. Two-thirds of the world's fresh water is stored in glaciers. Their melting leaves poor countries with less of a buffer to protect farmers against changing weather and rain-fall patterns.

This kind of increasing unpredictability would be dire news at the best of times: hit by drought and flood, the land becomes less productive. It is compounded by another problem. The higher-yielding, pest-resistant seed varieties invented in the 1960s were designed to thrive in stable climes. Old-fashioned seeds are actually better at dealing with variable weather—but are now less widely used. Reinstituting their use will mean less food.

In India the gains from the Green Revolution are already shrinking because of local pollution, global warming and waning resistance to pests and disease. A study for the Massachusetts Institute of Technology forecast that yields of the main Indian crops would decline by a further 4.5–9% over the next 30 years because of climate change. A recent assessment based on a large number of studies of what might happen in the long run if carbon continues to be pumped into the atmosphere found that world farm production could fall by 16% by the 2080s, and possibly by as much as 21% in developing countries. Although the timescale makes such figures no more than educated guesses, there is not much doubt that climate change is undermining the gains from intensive farming in developing countries—at the very time when population growth and greater wealth mean the world will need to double food production over the next three or four decades. By 2050 the world will have to feed 2 billion to 3 billion more people and cope with the changing (water-hungry) diets of a richer population. Even without climate change, farm productivity would have to rise by 1% a year, which is a lot. With climate change, the rise will have to be 1.8%, says the bank.

If these myriad problems have a silver lining, it is that they give developing countries as big an interest in mitigating the impact of climate change as rich ones. As the World Bank says, climate-change policy is no longer a simple choice between growth and ecological well-being.

[I]f carbon continues to be pumped into the atmosphere ... world farm production could fall by 16% by the 2080s, and possibly by as much as 21% in developing countries.

Sideways to Copenhagen

In principle that shift should make a climate-change deal in Copenhagen more likely, by increasing the number of countries that want an agreement. But two big problems remain. First, the poor countries want large amounts of money. To keep global warming down to an increase of 2°C [36°F], the World Bank calculates, would cost $140 billion to $675 billion a year in developing countries—dwarfing the $8 billion a year now flowing to them for climate-change mitigation. The $75 billion cost of adapting to global warming (as opposed to trying to stop it) similarly overwhelms the $1 billion a year available to them.

Second, poor countries see a climate-change deal in fundamentally different terms. For rich countries the problem is environmental: greenhouse gases are accumulating in the atmosphere and must be cut, preferably using the sort of binding targets recommended by the Intergovernmental Panel on Climate Change. For developing countries the problem is one of fairness and history: rich countries are responsible for two-thirds of the carbon put into the atmosphere since 1850; to cut emissions in absolute terms now would perpetuate an unjust pattern. Poor countries therefore think emissions per head, not absolute emissions, should be the standard.

Moreover, targets set at national level have little effect in poor countries where public administration works badly. So rich and poor also disagree about the conditions attached to any money for mitigating or adapting to climate change. The rich see this as a sort of aid, designed for specific projects with measurable targets, requiring strict conditions. Poorer countries see the cash as no-strings compensation for a problem that is not of their making.

The cost of climate change gives developing countries a big interest in a deal at Copenhagen. But what sort of deal they want—and how hard they push for it—is another matter altogether.

8

Climate Change
Must Be Addressed in
Developed Countries

Curtis Doebbler

Based in Washington, DC, Curtis Doebbler is a renowned international human rights lawyer.

Led by the United States, developed countries stand in the way of actions to fight and respond to climate change. While obstructing minimal emissions limits, rich states attempt to place the burden of global carbon reduction on poor states. Developed countries contribute very little to the enormous costs of mitigation and adaptation, and their representatives in climate talks refuse to extend and strengthen emissions limits, contrary to those of developing countries. Likewise, the carbon-trading system allows rich states to buy the rights to pollute from poor states, which not only fails to reduce greenhouse gasses, but also keeps global wealth and economic growth centered in developed nations, subjecting developing nations to the harms of climate change.

Climate change is widely acknowledged to be the greatest threat facing humanity. It will lead to small island states disappearing from the face of the earth, serious global threats to our food and water supplies, and ultimately the death of hundreds of millions of the poorest people in the world over the course of this century.

Curtis Doebbler, "Two Threats to Our Existence," *Al-Ahram Weekly Online*, 1055, July 7–13, 2011. Reproduced by permission

No other threat—including war, nuclear disasters, rogue regimes, terrorism, or the fiscal irresponsibility of governments—is reliably predicted to cause so much harm to so many people on earth, and indeed to the earth itself. The International Panel on Climate Change, which won the Nobel Prize for its evaluation of thousands of research studies to provide us accurate information on climate change, has predicted that under the current scenario of "business-as-usual", temperatures could rise by as much as 10 degrees Celsius [18 degrees Fahrenheit] in some parts of the world. This would have horrendous consequences for the most vulnerable people in the world. Consequences that the past spokesman of 136 developing countries, Lumumba Diaping, described as the equivalent of sending hundreds of millions of Africans to the furnace.

Yet for more than two decades, states have failed to take adequate action to either prevent climate change or to deal with its consequences. A major reason for this is that many wealthy industrialised countries view climate change as at worst an inconvenience, or at best even a potential market condition from which they can profit at the expense of developing countries. Indeed, history has shown them that because of their significantly higher levels of population they have grown rich and been able to enslave, exploit and marginalise their neighbours in developing countries. They continue in this vein.

Standing in the Way of Action

Still, government representatives, led by the United States and other developed countries, continue to stand in the way of even the most basic action. They are blocking legally-binding minimally adequate emissions limits with the result that temperature rises are inevitable and will cause deadly harm to people in many developing countries, and will eventually destroy the planet. Ironically, these same rich countries are calling for developing countries to carry the greatest burden of cutting emissions. If developing countries were to shoulder this burden this would lead to an even greater difference in living standards between the world's richest and the poorest. But it is unlikely they could even do so if they wanted to carry such a disproportional burden. The reason is that they have neither the technology that is needed to cut emissions without literally killing their people and the richest countries and private entities therein that have the technology are not willing to share it.

> *[I]t is getting harder for developed countries to ignore the "ticking clock" of climate change that has already condemned many people in the Global South to lives of misery.*

As if to rub salt into the wounds of the developing countries facing the inevitability of climate destruction, the developed countries are also refusing to provide even a fraction of the estimated resources needed to carry this burden and at the same time protect their people. It is true that the resources needed to stop the planet from overheating and to protect people from the climate change that we can already not prevent is not a small sum of money. According to the World Bank, it is as much as $750 billion a year at 2009 rates—today over $1 trillion in light of the collapsing US dollar. To date, developed countries have made a top offer of $30 billion now and 100 billion by 2020. In fact, they have put more effort into mysteriously revising the World Bank figure downwards while the costs of the actions needed have risen and the damage already done has increased. Still, despite offering too little and fiddling the books to decrease the amount that they need to offer, developing countries have disbursed less than one per cent of even their inadequate pledges.

It would seem to be a classic case of the rich just not caring about the poor. Indeed, they don't seem to need to care. Developed countries seem to have such disproportionate financial resources advantages that they can even purchase the support of developing countries. The tiny island archipelago of Maldives, which will already most certainly disappear because of the rising sea levels caused by climate change, has, for example, given up on trying to take adequate action on climate change. Instead, it frequently supports the proposals of developed countries to take inadequate action. In 2009, its president publicly declared at the annual climate talks that he could agree to nothing better than a deal that would lead to his country disappearing under the sea. Whether the words were his or actually those of developed countries is unclear, as his speaking points are sometimes written by advisors who are paid and made available to the Maldives by rich developed countries.

Regardless, it is getting harder for developed countries to ignore the "ticking clock" of climate change that has already condemned many people in the Global South to lives of misery. The year 2010 was a stark reminder when average global temperatures reached their highest level ever and natural disasters became regular occurrences.

Another Year of Fruitless Talk

Nevertheless, while our atmosphere is literally burning up around us, our representatives talk, but take no effective action. The recent climate talks in Bonn, Germany that ended [in June 2011] were supposed to lay the groundwork for an agreement on adequate international action at the next major round of global talks in Durban, South Africa from 28 November to 9 December 2011. In Durban, ministers and heads of states and governments will come together to decide whether action can be taken to ensure we cut our global emissions of greenhouse gases. If they don't agree to extend and increase their obligations to cut emissions under the Kyoto Protocol to the UN Framework Convention on Climate Change (UNFCCC), the obligations for states to take the action that is needed most urgently to combat climate change will end in 2012.

In Bonn, developed countries stood obstinately against extending these emission limits. The United States, which is the only major emitting country that never joined the Kyoto Protocol, as well as Canada and Japan, stated publicly that they would not agree to extend the Kyoto Protocol even before the latest round of meetings began. These developed states took this stance despite that fact that almost all other states want to extend and strengthen the emission limits in the Kyoto Protocol. They just do not seem to care.

At a briefing for US NGOs [non-governmental organization], the US chief negotiator in Bonn, Jonathan Perishing, offered incredible excuses for his country's intransigence. They ranged from domestic law to excuses cowered in the language of long discredited climate sceptics. The biggest problem, however, was perhaps that neither he nor his significant number of colleagues seemed to care. In typical American fashion, he concluded that it was about image and how the US gets its message across, rather than the fact that the consequences of its message are likely to be deadly for hundreds of millions of the most vulnerable people in the world. For the Americans and some of their allies, the lack of progress was to be viewed with satisfaction.

Some incremental progress was made; a few brackets were removed, a few words were agreed upon, but in the end just as much was left to disagreement as existed before the meetings. Moreover, on the most important issues states seemed even farther apart than when they started the negotiations. They were so far apart, that just like in meetings that took place in Bangkok last year [in 2010], they spent almost half their time discussing the agenda.

It was left to the permanent secretary of the small Solomon Islands' Ministry of Environment to remind delegates in the final meeting that they needed to act quickly because climate change is likely the greatest threat to the planet and human survival. But after a short ovation, as if to recognise the intrinsic wisdom of these words, delegates returned to the squabbling over details that has lasted almost two decades.

As delegates filtered out of the room, and even the executive secretary of the UNFCCC, Costa Rican Christina Figueres, could be seen walking hastily from the hall, a few of the almost silenced voices of civil society were given the opportunity to echo the call for urgent action. These NGOs pleaded for action and assessed the proceedings as providing much too little, much too late. These voices often emphasised the enhanced obligations of developed states under the international law. These obligations, as stated in the UNFCCC that has been ratified by 194 states, include the principle of "common but differentiated responsibilities" whereby an enhanced burden is placed on developed countries to do more to protect the climate. In Bonn, this principle seemed forgotten.

Failure to Act

To date, states have failed to take adequate action to prevent even the worst adverse effects of climate change. This failure is most pointedly evident in the failure of states to renew and enhance their legal and binding obligations to cut emissions of pollutants that cause climate change. Even states such as Canada and Japan who are party to the Kyoto Protocol have stated their clear intention to violate that treaty. They have done so by publicly declaring their intention not to extend its emission limits, despite the fact that Article 3, Paragraph 9, unambiguously requires the states party to the Kyoto Protocol to establish new limits after 2012 when the current limits expire.

In fact, most of the states with obligations under the Kyoto Protocol have not cut their emissions even by the modest—and widely acknowledged inadequate—requirements of that treaty. Many states will increase their overall emissions, but will be able to cloak their deficient action by buying the right to pollute from poorer states that do not have the capacity to pollute as much. This system of so-called "carbon trading" is allowing more pollution, instead of achieving the goal of the UNFCCC, which is to prevent the accumulation of dangerous levels of greenhouse gases in the atmosphere and thus curb the acceleration of climate change caused by human beings.

Many states will increase their overall emissions, but will be able to cloak their deficient action by buying the right to pollute from poorer states that do not have the capacity to pollute as much.

In other words, states are allowed to buy the right to pollute from poorer states. It is akin to a licence to kill sold by poorer states struggling to achieve minimal development. The tragic irony of this system is that it keeps the world's wealth and development in the richer developed states, while the people who will suffer the most from the adverse impacts of climate change are found in the poorer developing states. Again, in Bonn, the majority of developing states either refused to abide by their legal obligation to extend the Kyoto Protocol's emission limits or affirmatively stated that they had no intention to do so. A minority of these states, mainly European, did reiterate their willingness to extend the emission limits in the Kyoto Protocol, but they did not move much closer to actually doing so. Instead, they conditioned their promise to do something that they are already legally obliged to do on concessions from developing countries to a new regime.

Even when China agreed to cuts its emission by 45 per cent and India by 20 per cent to 25 per cent, something they have no legal obligation to do, the developed states refused to commit to an unconditional extension of strengthened emission limits in the Kyoto Protocol. The consequence is that the developed states that pollute the most can continue to do so and again have failed to take adequate action to control or mitigate climate change.

Moreover, this failure of to act has been complimented, and its adverse impacts intensified, by the failure to pay for adaptation or the action needed by poorer, developing states that will be more affected. These states need resources to protect their people against climate change. It sometimes means money, but also that developed states and private industry therein will allow developing states to exploit the technology that is currently denied to them by an onerous system of intellectual property that disproportionately favours wealthy countries, companies, and individuals.

Total Disaster Just Ahead

The lamentable picture is further exacerbated by the effort of developed states to prevent even loosely related action that may force them to take adequate action on climate change.

There have been several recent examples of action by developed states to remove from the agenda of the UN Human Rights Council (UNHRC) issues that could weaken their positions in climate talks. In the March meeting of the UNHRC, Switzerland convinced the tiny Maldives Islands to put forward what looked like a harmless resolution on the environment. The effect of the resolution, as a Swiss diplomat explained, was to turn back the clock on the action being taken by UNHRC on climate change. The British advisor to the Maldives further explained that climate change should not be on the agenda of the council. Indeed, if it were, then the human consequences of climate change would become more apparent and saving a few dollars instead of hundreds of millions of Africans lives might be less tolerated.

Especially rich developed countries appear increasingly embarrassed by their legacy of polluting our planet.

More recently, Norway brought together Nigeria and Argentina (coordinator of the Group of 77, which in fact represents 136 developing countries) to get them to push for ending the UNHRC's mandate on "Human Rights and Transnational Corporations and Business". Norway was well aware that their effort would prevent a mandate holder from being in place to raise the issue of the important contributions of private enterprise to climate change at the Durban meeting. In fact, the Norwegian-led move, which came after a recommendation for the appointment of a special representative of the secretary-general had already been made by ambassadors from all five regional groups, seemed mainly intended to again obscure the adverse human consequences of climate change that are caused by developed states.

As climate change affects people in almost every part of the world, it is not surprising that states have devised strategies to confront it in numerous different forums. Especially rich developed countries appear increasingly embarrassed by their legacy of polluting our planet. They have, however, chosen to deal with this guilt not by action, but by conscious inaction. It would appear as if they believe that they can bury the past and the present under the very ground that we commonly share. They may not have calculated, however, how dangerous such narrow-minded thinking may be for all of us.

9

Business Must Adapt to Climate Change

Tom Zeller Jr.

Tom Zeller Jr. is a senior writer at the Huffington Post *and a former reporter and editor at the* New York Times.

Profiting from global warming is a politically incorrect idea, but the business case for adapting to climate change is gaining support—even in the most affected areas. Businesses can benefit from assisting vulnerable communities they rely on for labor, crops, or materials—and strengthen growth markets in developing nations—by building up their infrastructures and safeguarding access to water, power, and other resources. But very few companies and corporations today integrate the risks and benefits of climate change in their business models and are reluctant to make such investments because of the uncertainty of global-warming data and impacts. Nonetheless, shifting weather patterns and intensified storms are inevitable.

Marc Karell, a climate change and environmental services consultant based in Mamaroneck, N.Y., recalled a lecture he delivered not long ago to a group of industrial environmental managers.

"I told them that one aspect of a warming climate will be its impacts on public health," Karell said in a recent phone call. "A warmer planet means that mosquitoes will be able to fly in a wider range around the equator than they can now, and therefore, they'll have access to hundreds of millions more people who were not exposed to it previously."

A member of the audience whose company manufactures and sells equipment that deals with malaria in the developing world, raised his hand. "You could see the lightbulb going off over his head," Karell said. "The guy said, 'If we're going to have more malaria, we could sell this stuff in so many more places,'—and then he put his hand over his mouth," Karell recalled, "realizing that he'd just said something that was probably very, very politically incorrect."

A growing chorus of advocates, consultants and organizations—including some toiling in areas likely to be hardest hit by global warming—are now arguing that such embarrassment needs to stop. "This is, after all, what business is all about—reacting to change, Karell said. "A good company prepares for, reacts to and takes advantage of change."

In other words, while high-profile investments in technologies and policies aimed at curbing global warming have grown significantly over the last decade (total global investment in clean energy topped $240 billion in 2010, according to Bloomberg New Energy Finance, a new high and more than four times the $51 million invested in 2004), such efforts, no matter how successful, won't be enough to halt changes that are likely already underway.

That doesn't mean investments and policies aimed at curbing emissions, transitioning to cleaner fuels and implementing efficiency programs ought to be abandoned. Former [US] vice president Al Gore, for example, argued in a sweeping essay published Wednesday [June 22, 2011] *Rolling Stone* that far greater progress on that front has been relentlessly sabotaged by "Polluters and Ideologues" who are are "trampling all over the 'rules' of democratic discourse."

"They are financing pseudoscientists whose job is to manufacture doubt about what is true and what is false," Gore continued, "buying elected officials wholesale with bribes that the politicians themselves have made 'legal' and can now be made in secret; spending hundreds of millions of dollars each year on misleading advertisements in the mass media; hiring four anticlimate lobbyists for every member of the U.S. Senate and House of Representatives."

Adaptation Makes Good Business Sense

Still, ardent advocates for combating, climate change, including Gore, know that the planet doesn't wait for dithering politicians and that the climate is already changing—and will continue to do so.

Crass as it sounds, there's plenty of money to be made in adapting to those changes, too—and plenty to be lost by ignoring it.

As suggested by a new report published jointly this week by the United Nations, the World Resources Institute and Oxfam America, these are points that precious few companies, both in the U.S. and around the globe, have yet to fully grasp.

Crass as it sounds, there's plenty of money to be made in adapting to [climate change]—and plenty to be lost by ignoring it.

The report, "Adapting for a Green Economy: Companies, Communities and Climate Change," took the pulse of dozens of companies that, as signatories to a U.N.-sponsored compact committing them to addressing climate change, are already considered to be at the forefront of the issue. The survey included such prominent names as Coca-Cola and DuPont, the American chemical giant, as well as dozens of foreign companies including Swiss Re, the global reinsurance firm, and the China National Offshore Oil Corporation, one of that country's three main national oil companies.

And yet while 83 percent of the firms that responded to the survey said they believed that climate change impacts posed a risk to their products or service—and a full 86 percent said climate change risks, or investing in adaptation solutions, pose a business opportunity—precious few could articulate ways in which they'd integrated adaptation risks and potential rewards into their business models.

Why does this matter? Well, despite relentless efforts in this country among polluters and their friends in Congress to forestall ambitious energy and climate policy, new regulations in various parts of the world are inevitable. A recent economic analysis by the investment consulting firm Mercer suggested that "the economic cost of climate policy for the market to absorb is estimated to amount to as much as approximately $8 trillion cumulatively, by 2030."

And while public policy will inevitably be the main driver in addressing those areas likely to be hardest hit by global warming, businesses also have a major role to play in helping some of the planet's most vulnerable communities weather the worst of it—from rising seas to scorched crops and diminished fresh water supplies, among other potential effects.

"Community risks are business risks," said Heather Coleman, a senior policy advisor on climate change at Oxfam and a contributor to this week's new report. "When there's a massive flood in Pakistan, for instance, those communities in many respects represent the labor force for some global companies, and crops that companies are sourcing there, the yield is demolished. Companies are not immune to these risks."

It only makes good business sense then, the report argues, to help those communities shore up roads and other critical infrastructure; to fortify ports, railroads and airports; and to ensure that access to critical resources like water and power are resilient to potential changes.

Samantha Putt del Pino, a co-director for business engagement in climate and technology at the World Resources Institute, added that the healthier and more resilient these communities are, the more likely they will become prosperous markets themselves.

"If you take a look at Fortune Global 500, they talk about their growth markets, but if you look at where that growth market is—it's in those developing nations," Putt del Pino said. If those populations are not resilient, companies are losing the very areas they are depending on for their future growth."

That should be a clarion call for groups like the U.S. Chamber of Commerce, the nation's main business lobby, which has long argued—albeit with the intent of beating back what it considered burdensome climate policy—that communities are well positioned to adapt to climate change.

Problem is, it's hard to divorce businesses from the communities that work for them, supply them with raw materials, buy their products and use their services.

Few Integrate Climate Change into Corporate Cultures

Some companies are beginning to get it. Coca-Cola, for example, has invested in a partnership linking over 50,000 small farmers in Uganda and Kenya, creating "a network of local suppliers for their fruit juices," according to the report. 'This grants communities access to market opportunities and diversified incomes, while at the same time creating a more robust and productive local supply chain for Coca-Cola.

CEMEX, the Mexican building materials and cement supplier, the report noted, is "actively working to develop more resilient and affordable housing for low-income communities, which are often the most vulnerable to climate change."

But these efforts remain isolated from the larger business models under which companies operate, Coleman said. Indeed, there were so few good examples of companies truly integrating the potential risks and rewards of climate change into their corporate cultures, that few case studies were available for citing.

What gives? Among other things, companies in the latest survey said they remain confused by the volume of long-term scientific data relating to climate risks, and how best to integrate that into decisions relating to operations on the ground in specific locations. Others said continued uncertainty over future climate impacts made taking investment risks difficult, as did the inherently long-delayed return on such investments, which will inevitably be measured in decades, even if the need for investment is now.

The need for investment is most certainly now—and the wisdom Coleman, Putt del Pino and their co-authors attempt to impart applies equally to companies whose supply chains don't necessarily reach Bangladesh.

Coleman pointed to the American energy firm Entergy as a standout example of a firm that gets it—having watched some of the southern communities it serves get battered over the last several years by hurricanes and floods of increased frequency and intensity. The company commissioned a report to look at the potential economic risks of climate change along the Gulf Coast. That report, published last fall, concluded among other things that over the next 20 years, the Gulf Coast could face cumulative economic damages reaching as high as $350 billion. "In the 2030 timeframe, hurricane Katrina/Rita-type years of economic impact may become a once in every generation event as opposed to once every ˜100 years today," the report stated.

Extreme Weather Will Become More Common

But even with evidence of shifting and more violent weather appearing to swirl and simmer before our very eyes—at home and abroad—many companies remain fixated on the status quo.

Sure, reasonable people hold differing opinions on what any one storm or season suggests. But there's little doubt that, over the coming decades, such weather is likely to become more common.

But even with evidence of shifting and more violent weather appearing to swirl and simmer before our very eyes—at home and abroad—many companies remain fixated on the status quo.

"The last couple months we've been hearing a lot more about risks and adaptation," said Karell, the environmental consultant from New York. "You've got wildfires out West and flooding in the South and there's just a lot more of it occurring, and the public is starting to put the dots together. And at some point, companies are going to have to say, 'Gee, this is going to impact my business. I may not be able to get my widgets to market.'"

10

Involving Business in the Fight Against Climate Change Is Problematic

Bjørn Lomborg

Based in Denmark, Bjørn Lomborg is an adjunct professor at the Copenhagen Business School, director of think tank Copenhagen Consensus Center, and author of The Skeptical Environmentalist.

When global-warming activists and big business join to fight climate change, the self-interests of energy companies, lobbyists, and other players in the green movement must be taken into account. Activists and businesses drum up support for expensive climate-change policies from which they stand to gain, but have little impact on global warming. Energy industry corporations, for example, tout green "credentials" while profiting from oil or gas sales, and advocates promote biofuels despite their negative impact on the environment and food prices. Ultimately, the merger of interests between activists and businesses lead to ineffective and costly approaches to climate change.

In May [2011], the United Nations' International Panel on Climate Change [IPCC] made media waves with a new report on renewable energy. As in the past, the IPCC first issued a short summary; only later would it reveal all of the data. So it was left up to the IPCC's spin-doctors to present the take-home message for journalists.

Bjørn Lomborg, "Green Bootleggers and Baptists," *Project Syndicate*, July 15, 2011. http://www.project-syndicate.org. Reproduced by permission.

The first line of the IPCC's press release declared, "Close to 80% of the world's energy supply could be met by renewables by mid-century if backed by the right enabling public policies." That story was repeated by media organizations worldwide.

Last month [June 2011], the IPCC released the full report, together with the data behind this startlingly optimistic claim. Only then did it emerge that it was based solely on the most optimistic of 164 modeling scenarios that researchers investigated. And this single scenario stemmed from a single study that was traced back to a report by the environmental organization Greenpeace. The author of that report—a Greenpeace staff member—was one of the IPCC's lead authors.

The claim rested on the assumption of a large reduction in global energy use. Given the number of people climbing out of poverty in China and India, that is a deeply implausible scenario.

When the IPCC first made the claim, global-warming activists and renewable-energy companies cheered. "The report clearly demonstrates that renewable technologies could supply the world with more energy than it would ever need," boasted Steve Sawyer, Secretary-General of the Global Wind Energy Council.

This sort of behavior—with activists and big energy companies uniting to applaud anything that suggests a need for increased subsidies to alternative energy—was famously captured by the so-called "bootleggers and Baptists" theory of politics.

The theory grew out of the experience of the southern United States, where many jurisdictions required stores to close on Sunday, thus preventing the sale of alcohol. The regulation was supported by religious groups for moral reasons, but also by bootleggers, because they had the market to themselves on Sundays. Politicians would adopt the Baptists' pious rhetoric, while quietly taking campaign contributions from the criminals.

Of course, today's climate-change "bootleggers" are not engaged in any illegal behavior. But the self-interest of energy companies, biofuel producers, insurance firms, lobbyists, and others in supporting "green" policies is a point that is often missed.

Supported by Activists, Cheered on by Businesses

Indeed, the "bootleggers and Baptists" theory helps to account for other developments in global warming policy over the past decade or so. For example, the Kyoto Protocol would have cost trillions of dollars, but would have achieved a practically indiscernible difference in stemming the rise in global temperature. Yet activists claimed that there was a moral obligation to cut carbon-dioxide emissions, and were cheered on by businesses that stood to gain.

During the ill-fated Copenhagen climate summit in December 2009, Denmark's capital city was plastered with slick ads urging the delegates to make a strong deal—paid for by Vestas, the world's largest windmill producer.

Oil tycoon T. Boone Pickens, a famous convert to environmentalism, drafted a "plan" (which he named after himself) to increase America's reliance on renewables. Of course, he would also have been one of the major investors in the wind-power and natural-gas companies that would benefit from government subsidies.

Traditional energy giants like BP [British Petrol] and Shell have championed their "green" credentials, while standing to profit from selling oil or gas instead of environmentally "unfriendly" coal. Even US electricity giant Duke Energy, a major coal consumer, won green kudos for promoting a US cap-and-trade scheme. But the firm ended up opposing the draft legislation to create such a scheme, because it did not provide sufficient free carbon-emission permits for coal companies.

Dubious claims by faithful activists gave rise to the biofuels industry (with supporting lobbyists). Biofuel production likely *increases* atmospheric carbon, owing to the massive deforestation that it requires, while crop diversion increases food prices and contributes to global hunger. While environmentalists have started to acknowledge this, the industry received a lot of activist support when it began—and neither agribusiness nor green-energy producers have any interest in changing course now.

Whenever opposite political forces attract, as activists and big business have in the case of global warming, there is a high risk that the public interest will be caught in the middle.

Obviously, private firms are motivated by self-interest, and that is not necessarily a bad thing. But, too often, we hear commentators suggest that when Greenpeace and Big Business agree on something, it must be a sensible option. Business support for expensive policies such as the Kyoto Protocol—which would have done very little for climate change—indicate otherwise.

The climate-change "Baptists" provide the moral cover that politicians can use to sell regulation, along with scary stories that the media can use to attract readers or viewers. Businesses see opportunities for taxpayer-funded subsidies, and to pass on inevitable cost growth to consumers.

Unfortunately, this convergence of interests can push us to focus on ineffective, expensive responses to climate change. Whenever opposite political forces attract, as activists and big business have in the case of global warming, there is a high risk that the public interest will be caught in the middle.

11

Climate Change and Water

United Nations World Water Assessment Programme

Coordinated and lead by the United Nations Educational, Scientific, and Cultural Organization (UNESCO), the United Nations World Water Assessment Programme (WAPP) monitors global freshwater supplies.

Climate change has enormous implications on water supplies, threatening global security as dependence between nations grows. Global warming is expected to alter the pattern of precipitation and other water cycles—affecting agriculture, freshwater availability, droughts, and flooding—and mitigation may have negative effects on water resources and demand. Furthermore, water scarcity can turn competition into conflict and violence in unstable areas. Adaptation to climate change must include investments and innovations in water systems, infrastructures, and policies. These measures are an opportunity to counter the instabilities caused by climate change and water scarcity, particularly in vulnerable nations.

Climate change, especially its implications for scarce water resources, is a matter of collective security in a fragile and increasingly interdependent world. At a 2007 United Nations (UN) Security Council debate on the impact of climate change on peace and security, UN Secretary-General Ban Ki-moon noted that climate change has implications for peace and security, as well as serious implications for the environment, societies and economies. In particular, he stressed that this is es-

United Nations World Water Assessment Programme, "3. Responses to Climate Change Must Focus on Water," *Climate Change and Water*, New York: United Nations World Water Assessment Programme, 2009, pp. 10–13. Reproduced by permission.

pecially the case 'in vulnerable regions that face multiple stresses at the same time—pre-existing conflict, poverty and unequal access to resources, weak institutions, food insecurity and incidence of diseases such as HIV/AIDS'. He outlined 'alarming, though not alarmist' scenarios, including limited or threatened access to energy increasing the risk of conflict; a scarcity of food and water transforming peaceful competition into violence; and floods and droughts sparking massive human migrations, polarizing societies and weakening the ability of countries to resolve conflicts peacefully. In Africa alone, by 2020, 75–250 million people may be exposed to increased water stress due to climate change.

Adverse changes in internal, interjurisdictional and transboundary waters can put food, social, health, economic, political and military security at risk. Some fragile states have experienced widespread conflict that has resulted in the destruction of economic infrastructure. The vulnerability of affected populations is worsened by the state's loss of control over the forces of law and order and ultimately by its loss of political legitimacy.

Investing in water systems and services is an opportunity to counter these destabilizing forces. Widespread conflict in some fragile states has destroyed much of their social and economic infrastructure. Restoring this, and renewing their institutional capacity, can help to set post-conflict nations on a path to recovery. For example, the rehabilitation of damaged irrigation infrastructure and expansion of water supply and sanitation was a key feature of the 2006 Somali Rehabilitation and Reconstruction Plan. Rebuilding after major natural disasters is also an opportunity to address long-standing infrastructure deficits.

The Vulnerability of Populations

One of the most pressing challenges that climate change brings is the vulnerability of populations, especially the poor among them, to the impacts of extreme events such as floods, storm surges and droughts. The rural poor, usually the most vulnerable and the most dependent on reliable environmental resources, represent about half of the world's population today, or 3.3 billion people. While trends indicate that by 2030, urban dwellers will make up about 60% of the world's population, a large proportion of the other 40% will continue to rely on subsistence and rainfed agriculture for their livelihoods. Climate change is likely to intensify existing pressures, increasing risk, vulnerability and uncertainty. Over the longer term, incremental climate change will impinge on decisions about food security, energy security and land use, all with implications for the management of water resources and environmental sustainability.

Many regions are not yet taking the need to store more water into account, resulting in a growing frequency of local crises during extreme drought.

The number of countries and regions without enough water to produce their food is rising as populations increase. Meeting water needs during dry seasons and ensuring security of supply require water storage. Climate change will intensify climate irregularity, so that more storage will be needed to ensure the same level of security. More water will have to be kept in reservoirs as reserves for dry spells, leaving less for everyday use. But this increased need for storage is occurring at a time when pressure from users is forcing water managers to take risks and reduce carryover stocks. Many regions are not yet taking the need to store more water into account, resulting in a growing frequency of local crises during extreme drought.

While in many developed countries water storage at a level of 70%–90% ensures reliable sources of water for irrigation, water supply and hydropower, as well as a buffer for flood management, less developed countries, such as those in Africa, for example, store as little as 4% of annual renewable flows, risking serious vulnerabilities in the short and longer term.

Developing countries need support of all kinds, including financial, to improve climatic adaptation, which affects development at many levels. In Africa, the impacts of climate change are expected to range from increased energy shortages, reduced agricultural production, worsening food security and malnutrition to the increasing spread of disease, more humanitarian emergencies, growing migratory pressures and increased risks of conflict over scarce land and water resources. Finance for adaptation should be augmented and made available for programmes in all sectors where this is likely to be required.

A More Urgent Need for Adaptation

There is an urgent need to mitigate the pressures on climate change, but meanwhile there is an even more urgent need to adapt to changes that are already under way. Adaptation measures must be taken in several crucial areas: food, energy, the environment and economic development: all deserve top priority and commensurate funding.

The intergovernmental response has focused primarily on mitigation of climate change, embracing wide-ranging measures including reducing greenhouse gas emissions, developing clean technologies and protecting forests. But although these measures may slow climate change, they will not halt or reverse it, and it will be two generations before they begin to have an effect. Even if successful, we face a considerably changed future climate.

People must be protected from the consequences of global climate change through adaptation measures.

Decisions and policies for mitigation (reducing greenhouse gas emissions, applying clean technologies and protecting forests) and adaptation (such as expansion of rain-water storage and water conservation practices) can have profound consequences on water supply and demand. Climate mitigation measures are not always beneficial for water resources, while some water management policies can even increase greenhouse gas emissions.

For example, many developed countries are shifting to 'clean' energy sources and away from thermal energy plants based on fossil fuels. But there is evidence that hydroelectric stations can generate large volumes of greenhouse gases released from sediment and decaying organic matter at the bottom of reservoirs. Even marginal land, for example that used by pastoralists and subsistence agriculturalists in Africa, is being targeted by developed countries for biofuel production. Water resource implications, as well as climate change impacts on these fragile ecosystems, must be fully taken into account so that win-win scenarios can be developed.

The First African Water Week, convened in Tunis in March 2008, opened with a call for greater efforts to ensure water security nationally and regionally. Donald Kaberuka, president of the African Development Bank Group, emphasized that 'it is no longer acceptable that the African continent continues to utilize only 4% of its water resources, when a huge proportion of the people do not have access to safe water, and when large populations are faced with frequent floods and drought, in addition to food and energy shortages. Action is urgently needed'.

Agriculture's Complex Relationship with Climate Change

Climate change is expected to alter hydrologic regimes (the pattern of precipitation, runoff, infiltration and evaporation affecting a water body) and the availability of freshwater, which will affect both rainfed and irrigated agriculture. There is increasing likelihood of reduced precipitation in semi-arid areas, more variable rainfall distribution, more frequent extreme events and rising temperatures, especially in low latitudes. A severe reduction in river runoff and aquifer recharge is expected in the Mediterranean basin and in the semi-arid areas of Southern Africa, Australia and the Americas, affecting the availability of water for all uses.

Agriculture is by far the largest consumer of freshwater. Globally, about 70% of freshwater withdrawals go to irrigated farming. Water scarcity may limit food production and supply, putting pressure on food prices and increasing countries' dependence on food imports. The number of countries and regions without enough water to produce their food is rising as populations increase.

There is increasing likelihood of reduced precipitation in semi-arid areas, more variable rainfall distribution, more frequent extreme events and rising temperatures . . .

Agriculture has a complex relationship with climate change. On the one hand, it adds to global warming through emissions of methane and other gases into the atmosphere. To mitigate this, changes in land use practices (management of cropland and grazing land) are considered to be the best options. On the other hand, agriculture is also likely to be seriously affected by climate change in different ways, depending on geographical and other factors. Large areas of croplands, in particular in semi-arid zones, will need to adapt to new conditions with lower precipitation.

The projected increase in the frequency of droughts and floods will affect the yield of crops and livestock. Though its net effect on food production at the global level is uncertain, climate change will alter the distribution of agricultural potential. Most of the increase in cereal production will be concentrated in the Northern Hemisphere, while local production could be affected, especially in subsistence sectors at low latitudes. Several densely populated farming systems in developing countries are at risk. A combination of reduced base flows from rivers, increased flooding and rising sea levels is expected to damage highly productive irrigated systems that help maintain the stability of cereal production. These production threats will be more significant in alluvial plains dependent on glacier melt (e.g. Colorado, or Punjab) and, in particular, in lowland deltas (the Ganges and Nile).

In key areas of food insecurity dominated by rainfed agriculture (sub-Saharan Africa and peninsular India, in particular), the expected reductions in production may have multiple impacts including loss of livelihoods and displacement of rural populations. This will accentuate demand in global markets and put further pressure on irrigated production. In large irrigation systems that rely on high mountain glaciers for water, such as the Andes, Himalayas and Rocky Mountains, temperature changes will cause high runoff periods to shift to earlier in the spring, when irrigation water demand is still low. Such changes could incite demand for new water-control infrastructure to compensate for changes in river runoff. Elsewhere, current farming and cropping systems may become unsustainable.

Adjusting to climate change is one amongst several major challenges facing agriculture in the coming decades. Other challenges include producing enough food and soft commodities to satisfy the growth of global populations, sharing scarce water and land with other growing use sectors, and acknowledging the ecological and environmental need for water supply. The use of water is also being judged increasingly by equity and efficiency criteria. In short, major reforms and changes in farmer behaviour are called for.

Technical Improvements

Technological improvements can occur at all levels and affect all types of irrigation systems. These are not necessarily new, expensive or sophisticated options, but rather ones that are appropriate to needs and respond to actual demands. They should also match the capacity of system managers and farmers, and the resources available for proper operation and maintenance. Technological innovation is likely in three broad categories:

1. At the irrigation system level: water level, flow control and storage management within surface irrigation systems on all scales.

2. On the farm: storage, reuse, water lifting (manual and mechanical) and precision application technologies, such as overhead sprinklers and localized irrigation.

3. Across sectors: multiple-use systems in rural areas and urban agriculture with wastewater.

The situation can be remedied in many developing countries by investing in water infrastructure and by developing markets, credit, agricultural technology and extension services. Making national water policies more coherent is the basic aim of Integrated Water Resources Management (IWRM), a leading paradigm used by those involved in determining water policy.

Direct and Indirect Approaches

The threat of climate change has led to many developments in the simulation of atmospheric processes, improving the accuracy of climate and weather forecasts. Combined with improved technology for monitoring, collecting and analyzing information, these developments should lead to improvements in warning systems for floods and droughts and other major water-related events. If these can be combined with hazard mitigation strategies involving all levels of affected communities, there are enormous opportunities to avoid loss of human life and economic damages. Other examples of potential hazards becoming opportunities include using increased runoff from glacial melting to develop more reliable water reserves. However, this solution will only be temporary and viable as long as the glaciers have not melted completely. In other countries, potential for increasing the reliability of water supplies exists through the use of flood water storage to increase the reliability and to improve floodplain management and planning.

Approaches to incorporating climate change information in decision-making can be either direct or indirect. *Direct approaches* incorporate climate change information into decision-making—for example, climate scientists interacting with partnering utilities to find space and time scales appropriate for adaptations to reduce the risk of climate extremes. *Indirect approaches* involve potentially affected people in studies of the readiness of societies to adapt to climate change. Although the indirect approach has dominated to date, the direct approach is likely to begin to predominate as water managers and decision-makers become more serious about adaptation to climate change.

Responses to the challenges of climate change are likely to be specific for each country or national region. . . . Bhutan is one example of a country that has coordinated its national water and climate change adaptation policies to meet short- and long-term threats of glacier lake outburst floods resulting from climate change-induced glacier melting. Another good example for policy integration is Tunisia.

High-income countries are experiencing water management problems that are very different from those of poor countries. While high-income countries can afford to pay more attention to the environment and to long-term water system sustainability, developing countries prioritize eliminating poverty and raising the overall level of health and well-being, sometimes at the expense of environmental sustainability. Conflict situations regarding water usage between agriculture and other demands will create additional challenges for water managers and policy makers.

Leaving the Way Open for Future Options

Given the uncertainties about climate change, decisions on current problems should leave the way open for future options. No-regrets strategies—actions that would significantly reduce the adverse impacts of change but would not cause harm if projections of impacts of change are wrong—are important in responding to climate change. In contrast, failure to act carries risks because the situation may deteriorate if no action is taken.

Developed countries and developing countries must work together to identify socioeconomic priorities and to invest in and use water to power the engines of growth. They must break cycles of poverty while avoiding the harmful environmental and health consequences of unbridled development experienced in many developed countries. Cooperation between developed countries and developing countries can build mitigation, adaptation, avoidance and no-regret measures into decision-making, to avoid incurring the costs of neglected environmental management later.

Where water is scarce, the challenge is to select the development path that attains the best social, economic and environmental outcomes.

It will be important to work toward reducing uncertainty, facilitate decision-making and accelerate investment by identifying the links between socioeconomic development, environmental sustainability, water management capacity and investments in water-related infrastructure and other sectors.

Options depend on social, economic and environmental conditions, the availability of water over space and time, and the threat of droughts and floods, all of which vary around the world. Where water is scarce, the challenge is to select the development path that attains the best social, economic and environmental outcomes. Such decisions shift the trade-offs away from water resources alone to broader concerns of environmental, economic and social benefits. Making decisions about water in this context can sometimes introduce inefficiencies in other development activities. For example, importing food rather than producing it domestically may permit water to be used for higher value outputs, but many farmers will then need to find other ways to earn a living.

12

Climate Change Adaptation Must Prioritize Food Security

IASC Task Force on Climate Change

The Inter-Agency Standing Committee (IASC) is an interagency forum of United Nations (UN) and non-UN humanitarian partners. Its Task Force on Climate Change was established in 2008.

Climate change threatens food security by increasing the frequency of natural disasters, limiting access to land and water, and hindering productivity. At greatest risk are the most vulnerable in developing nations and states, populations that are poor and already food insecure. There are four main strategies to ensure food security in the face of climate change: raising productivity, resilience, and sustainability in agriculture; improving disaster risk management, relief, and response; enhancing social protection systems and support; and fostering the development of resilient communities. Major advances in these areas are necessary to reduce hunger as climate change takes place.

Climate change directly affects food security and nutrition. It undermines current efforts to protect the lives and livelihoods and end the suffering of the over 1 billion food insecure people and will increase the risk of hunger and malnutrition by an unprecedented scale within the next decades. Undernutrition is already the single largest contributor to the global burden of disease, killing 3.5 million people every year,

IASC Task Force on Climate Change, "Climate Change, Food Insecurity, and Hunger," November 2009, pp. 1–7. Copyright © 2009 by the IASC. All rights reserved. Reproduced by permission.

almost all of them children in developing countries. Unless urgent action is taken, it will not be possible to ensure the food security of a growing world population under a changing climate. . . .

Existing Challenges to Food Security

In the last fifty years the world population has more than doubled: from 3 billion to 6.7 billion people. Over one billion of them are undernourished—an unacceptable situation and a big challenge to global efforts to end hunger and poverty. In the next forty years, world population will increase by another 50%, reaching more than 9 billion by 2050. Meeting the demand of such a large population will put enormous additional pressure on food production systems. Regardless of climate change, demand for food will increase, while resources needed for its production, such as land, water and petrol-based fertilizers—are becoming scarcer and scarcer. The risk of hunger is very likely to increase by a large extent in the next decades due to a number of factors described below—even if the climate was not changing.

Climate Change—a Multiplier of Food Security Risks

Climate change will act as a multiplier of existing threats to food security: It will make natural disasters more frequent and intense, land and water more scarce and difficult to access, and increases in productivity even harder to achieve. The implications for people who are poor and already food insecure and malnourished are immense.

Particularly in the least developed countries and small island developing states, it is the livelihoods and lives of the poorest and most vulnerable, including women, children and marginal communities, which are also at greatest risk to suffer from to the potential impacts of climate change. This is due to their high exposure to natural hazards, their direct dependence on climate-sensitive resources such as plants, trees, animals, water and land, and their limited capacity to adapt to and cope with climate change impacts. This ability depends to a large extend on the level of economic development and the means required for adaptation, such as economic entitlements, land, capital, credit and/or tenure rights. It also depends on institutional support and the possibility to influence decision-making.

Climate change will affect all four dimensions of food security: availability, accessibility, stability and utilisation. It will reduce food availability, because it negatively affects the basic elements of food production—soil, water and biodiversity. Rural communities face increased risks including recurrent crop failure, loss of livestock and reduced availability of fisheries and forest products. Changing temperatures and weather patterns furthermore create conditions for the emergence of new pests and diseases that affect animals, trees and crops. This has direct effects on the quality and quantity of yields as well as the availability and price of food, feed and fibre.

Climate change will affect all four dimensions of food security: availability, accessibility, stability, and utilisation.

At the same time, more extreme weather events will have serious impacts on livelihood assets in both rural and urban areas and threaten the stability of food supply. Many countries are already dealing with climate change impacts resulting from irregular, unpredictable rainfall patterns, increased incidence of storms and prolonged droughts. Decreasing availability of water and food will also increase sanitation and health problems and increase the risk of diseases and malnutrition. Competition over increasingly scarce resources will also increase the risk of conflicts, displacement and migration, which in turn will again increase the risk of food insecurity.

Reduced food availability due to decreasing yields as a result of climate change has additional direct implications for food accessibility: As food becomes scarce, prices go up and food becomes unaffordable, i.e. inaccessible, for a growing part of the population. The food price spike that peaked in 2008 clearly demonstrated how major fluctuations in global food markets can have far-reaching implications for food security and emergency relief needs. At the same time, the food price spike led to a dramatic increase in the global total of undernourished people by more than 20% to over a billion in July 2009. Some 125 million children are predicted to be underweight in 2010 if economies do not grow, 5 million more than if progress had continued at the 2007 rate. Even the pre-recession rate of improvement was inadequate to meet the MDG target. While prices fallen overall from the peak levels achieved in 2008, they are expected to remain on average 35 to 60% higher than in the past decade.

To the resulting increases in the number of people at risk of hunger, climate change is projected to add another 10 to 20% by 2050.

As outlined above, even without climate change further increases in food prices are expected. Recent modelling and analysis predicts additional price increases due to climate change for some of the most important agricultural crops—rice, wheat, maize, and soybeans. To the resulting increases in the number of people at risk of hunger, climate change is projected to add another 10 to 20% by 2050. Calorie availability in 2050 is likely to have declined relative to 2000 levels throughout the developing world: 24 million additional malnourished children, 21% more than today, are anticipated—almost half of them, 10 million, in sub-Saharan Africa.

Ensuring Food Security in a Changing Climate

There are four main entry points for adaptation and risk reduction strategies aiming at increased food security in view of climate change. Part of the solution is to increase food availability. Another lies in strategies that ensure that those who are at greatest risk of hunger can actually access and benefit from increased amounts of food and that protect the most vulnerable from the immediate impacts of climate change. This involves improving disaster risk management, enhancing social protection schemes (including the delivery of direct nutrition interventions) and strengthening resilient community-based development.

Increasing Agricultural Productivity, Resilience and Sustainability

Local people are the on-site land managers who play central roles in adapting agriculture and food systems to meet their needs under changing climate conditions. The concept of adapting to climate impacts is not new to them. Traditionally, coping mechanisms for adapting to seasonal and annual climate variability have included sharing local knowledge on varieties, farming systems, management technologies etc. But the need to increase production, coupled with the speed and magnitude of the expected changes in climate, poses new challenges.

Traditional coping mechanisms will not be sufficient to ensure food security and prevent effects on nutritional status. They must be complemented by the introduction of technical innovations and enabling frameworks. More research is needed on the breeding of new and adapted as well as the preservation of traditional, locally adapted varieties that can tolerate climate variability and are suitable for changed climatic conditions; the development of innovative but practical technologies such as alternative cropping systems, conservation and precision agriculture, and sustainable forest management; and the application and improvement of technologies for more efficient use of inputs such as energy, fertilizer, water, seeds. For all technological innovations in agriculture it is crucial that they will be easily accessible and affordable for the communities in need.

Adaptation strategies must also be supported by strong institutions and enabling policy and legal frameworks. Incentives and services for rural producers that can stimulate and guide adaptation processes and link producers to markets are also important supporting mechanisms. Adaptation to climate change can incorporate a range of successfully tested methods and technologies derived from sustainable agriculture and natural resource management and equitable and inclusive rural development approaches, building on the "no-regrets" principle. However, adaptation often involves substantial investments and changes in practices that may take a long time to implement or show benefits. It must therefore be complemented by other responses that address the immediate effects of climate change and protect those who cannot adapt.

Improving Disaster Risk Management

The number of people affected by disasters has more than tripled since the 1990s. In 2007 over 74 million people were victims of humanitarian crisis. As climate change leads progressively towards increased extremes—storms, droughts, and high temperatures—the challenge to the humanitarian community is not only to respond to the crises, but also to be better prepared and to be able to manage the risks more effectively.

Recent approaches that integrate relief and response in long-term risk management have begun to influence the way disaster management programs are planned and financed. In order to enhance community safety and resilience, the complex interactions between long-term risk reduction and short-term response need to be better understood. At the same time, the most vulnerable to food insecurity must be protected from the immediate impacts of climate change now.

Planning appropriate risk reduction and response requires an understanding of risks and vulnerabilities in terms of who are the vulnerable, where they are and why they are vulnerable. There is a need for improved monitoring, information systems and forward looking risk analysis. Particular efforts are needed to target the poorest and food insecure people without assets and entitlements in risk reduction or response interventions. In addition to a rural focus, attention has to be given to urban and peri-urban areas.

[T]he most vulnerable to food insecurity must be protected from the immediate impacts of climate change now.

As vulnerable people and communities themselves should always be the primary owners and drivers of any actions aimed at increasing their resilience to disasters, it is crucial to directly involve them in planning and implementation of disaster risk reduction. At the same time, in order to achieve greater effectiveness, disaster risk management and climate change adaptation management should also be linked and better integrated into national development plans and strategies, starting from poverty reduction strategies, food security strategies and sustainable development.

Moreover, the gaps between sectoral organizations must be bridged in order to share timely and relevant information concerning risks and their management. Climate information must be made accessible to affected communities and decision-makers. Last, but not least, sufficient financial resources are a prerequisite for effective disaster risk reduction.

Current practice indicates that less financial resources are being made available for disaster risk reduction than for adaptation.

Enhancing Social Protection Schemes

The existing inequities in food security, food safety and nutrition are likely to be further widened by the adverse consequences of climate change. Adapting food production systems has the potential to significantly increase the resilience of poor farmers to changing climate conditions. However, the vast majority of the 1 billion undernourished people do not have sufficient capacities and resources in order to adapt to or cope with the risks posed by climate change. They are in urgent need of public support in the form of social protection schemes, safety nets and other supportive measures.

Such public actions have large potential to increase resilience to climate change by contributing to breaking vicious cycles that lead into chronic poverty traps. Droughts, for example, frequently force poor families to sell off productive assets such as livestock; other shocks often lead to families taking children out of school and to reduction in households' food intake, number of meals, restriction of portion sizes, and purchase of less expensive but less nutritious foods—each with immediate and long-term physical and mental consequences for children. Eventual recovery becomes much more difficult as a result of such emergency "coping" measures. Environmental risks are among the most frequent, costly and impactful causes of such shocks—a problem that will grow immensely with climate change.

Social protection relevant to food insecurity, climate change and resource scarcity includes cash and in-kind transfers, such as Ethiopia's Productive Safety Net Programme, which transfers cash (and food) during seasonal food insecurity through employment on public works; employment guarantee schemes, which can be used to invest further in climate resilience, for example strengthening embankments or planting trees; Mother and Child Health and Nutrition and School Feeding programs; weather-indexed crop insurance; microfinance services; as well as emergency food assistance interventions. It also encompasses essential nutrition interventions, such as the distribution of micronutrient supplements for mothers and young children as well as fortification of foods as appropriate, and the treatment of severe acute malnutrition.

Access to formal social protection systems remains very limited in developing countries. At present only 20% of the world's people have access to formal social protection systems. Financing social protection support is complicated by the fact that safety nets need to be financed in a counter-cyclical manner, given that needs are greatest when economic performance is weakest. Effective targeting of the poorest and most vulnerable people is also critical, which fundamentally depends on policymakers understanding the vulnerabilities of these people. Apart from financial resources, formulating social protection policies hence demands significant institutional capacity, which international actors can help to build.

The many cases of degraded farms doubling production within a few years after adopting agro-ecological practices shows that such farms can 'jump' to a higher threshold . . . and greater resilience to current seasonal climatic stresses.

Strengthening Resilient Community-Based Development

Life-saving interventions to protect the food insecure people and their livelihoods from rapid-onset emergencies caused by climatic events are essential. It is equally important, however, to create enabling conditions to ensure that communities affected by disasters are able to build back systems which are better adapted to changing climate conditions. Supporting a transition towards "climate-smart" relief, rehabilitation and development that improves the livelihoods of low-income farmers and rural people and thereby increases their overall resilience must be considered the basis of adaptation.

Two thirds of developing country farmers farm on marginal lands, often on degraded soils. They form the majority of the food insecure and are most vulnerable to climate change. Yet experience shows the right strategies can transform their lives and create climate-resilient communities. Agro-ecological paths show enormous potential, if combined with equally crucial—and often neglected—strategies to empower farmers to influence policy formulation and implementation.

The many cases of degraded farms doubling production within a few years after adopting agro-ecological practices shows that such farms can 'jump' to a higher threshold, and enter a 'virtuous circle' of environmental restoration, renewed productivity, and greater resilience to current seasonal climatic stresses. Agro-ecological measures for delivering food security, climate change adaptation or mitigation typically deliver the other two objectives as well, delivering a "win-win-win" outcome. Achieving resilient communities, which involves people achieving increased material welfare and reduced risk, is bound up with people attaining greater capacity to determine their own destiny. Three factors are crucial: (a) The prospect of major new investment flows focused on previously neglected lands, (b) Incentivizing farmers through investments in agro-ecological practices and in providing environmental services, and (c) Communities influencing policy making and implementation.

Investments supporting community development in view of food security should target responsive institutions grounded in the local context; expanded and improved livelihood options; sound gender dynamics and full gender equality—

women must be integral to food security and resilience solutions; enhanced human capacity, building on local knowledge, and adequately connected with institutions at all levels, and creating a restored, diversified natural resource base.

An Unprecedented Challenge

Climate change poses an unprecedented challenge to the aim of eradicating hunger and poverty. In order to meet the growing demand for food security and nutrition under increasingly difficult climatic conditions and in a situation of diminishing resources, the world must urgently move towards embracing a two-fold approach: First, we must invest in and support the development of more efficient, sustainable and resilient food production systems. Second, we must improve access to adequate food and nutrition by the most vulnerable and at risk populations and communities and enhance social protection systems and safety nets as part of the adaptation agenda. Protecting the most vulnerable also requires enhancing our capacities to manage weather-related disaster risks and accelerating community development. Only if we succeed in making significant advances on all fronts—increasing food availability, enhancing access to food, and strengthening resilience and development—we will reduce the risk of dramatic increases in the number of hungry people among the poorest countries in the most vulnerable regions of the world.

Organizations to Contact

The editors have compiled the following list of organizations concerned with the issues debated in this book. The descriptions are derived from materials provided by the organizations. All have publications or information available for interested readers. The list was compiled on the date of publication of the present volume; the information provided here may change. Be aware that many organizations take several weeks or longer to respond to inquiries, so allow as much time as possible.

American Enterprise Institute (AEI)
1150 17th St. NW, Washington, DC   20036
(202) 862-5800 • fax: (202) 862-7177
website: www.aei.org

AEI is a public policy institute seeking to preserve and promote conservative values and public policy. The institute advocates for a government environmental policy that provides adequate protection for the environment without infringing on democratic institutions or human liberty. AEI dedicates a section of its website to publishing recent articles questioning the statement that "the science is settled" with regards to climate change. Additionally, articles critiquing current environmental policy are posted.

Cato Institute
1000 Massachusetts Ave., NW, Washington, DC   20001-5403
(202) 842-0200 • fax: (202) 842-3490
website: www.cato.org

The Cato Institute is an organization dedicated to espousing the libertarian principles of free market economics and limited government intervention in all areas of life. As such, Cato promotes energy and environmental policy that discourages government policies and incentives to push the development of sustainable energy sources, instead advocating for the free market's ability to provide the best solutions to environmental issues such as global warming. Current articles and studies by Cato concerning global warming are available online.

Center for the Study of Carbon Dioxide and Global Change
PO Box 25697, Tempe, AZ   85285-5697
(480) 966-3719
website: www.co2science.org

The Center for the Study of Carbon Dioxide and Global Change seeks to be a voice of scientific reason to counter what it dubs "alarmist global warming propaganda." The center provides scientific analysis of the rising levels of atmospheric carbon dioxide (CO_2) in its weekly online magazine *CO_2 Science*. Additionally, the organization posts online instructions for experiments that individuals can conduct in the classroom or at home to personally assess CO_2 enrichment and depletion.

Climate Reality Project
website: climaterealityproject.org

Founded and chaired by Al Gore, Nobel Laureate and former Vice President of the United States, the Climate Reality Project has more than 5 million members and supporters worldwide. The project believes that climate change is real and seeks to engage the public in discussing its challenges and solutions. The Climate Reality project website offers videos and other features on global warming, such as coverage of the global expeditions it sponsors.

Climate Skeptic
website: www.climate-skeptic.com

Run by Warren Meyer, the author of *A Skeptical Layman's Guide to Anthropogenic Global Warming*, this website contains articles and resources about global warming.

Daily Green
300 W. 57th St., New York, NY   10019
website: www.thedailygreen.com

Published by the Digital Media Unit of Hearst Magazines, the Daily Green considers itself a "consumers guide to the green revolution." The website posts news articles on environmental and climate change issues, as information on environmentally conscious homes and food, as well as eco-oriented quizzes, tips, and carbon calculators.

EarthShare

7735 Old Georgetown Rd., Suite 900, Bethesda, MD   20814
(800) 875-3863 • fax: (240) 333-0301
website: earthshare.org

EarthShare's mission is to engage individuals and organizations in creating a healthy environment. Among other activities, EarthShare supports a network of America's nonprofit conservation and environmental organizations and works to promote awareness and charitable giving through workplace giving campaigns. The organization also provides news and tips on environmental stewardship.

Environmental Defense Fund

257 Park Ave. South, New York, NY   10010
(212) 505-2100 • fax: (212) 505-2375
website: edf.org

EDF works to link science, economics and law to create innovative, equitable and cost-effective solutions to society's most urgent environmental problems. The website includes detailed information on the organization's work on global warming, endangered species, ocean-related issues, and other climate change and scientific concerns.

Green America

1612 K St. NW, Suite 600, Washington, DC   20006
(800) 584-7336
Website: www.greenamerica.org

Founded as Co-op America in 1982, Green America's mission is to create a socially just and environmentally sustainable society by using economic power. The organization focuses on economic strategies that can solve social and environmental problems. Green America also works to empower individuals to take both personal and collective action, and works to stop "abusive practices."

Green Living Ideas

website: greenlivingideas.com

Green Living Ideas provides tips, information, and ideas to help individuals "green" every area of their lives. Authors and experts weigh in with suggestions on how to lead an environmentally friendly lifestyle, covering such topics as fashion and beauty, home care, and travel.

Heartland Institute

One South Wacker Dr. #2740, Chicago, IL 60606
(312) 377-4000
website: heartland.org

The Heartland Institute's mission is to discover, develop, and promote free-market solutions to social and economic problems. The Institute promotes common-sense environmentalism and presents its ideas on how to best maintain a healthy environment. The site also has an archive of public-policy documents and links to their various publications.

Inter-Agency Standing Committee (IASC)
Task Force on Climate Change

IASC Secretariat, New York, NY 10017
(212) 963-5582
website: www.humanitarianinfo.org/iasc

The IASC is an interagency forum of United Nations (UN) and non-UN humanitarian partners. Established in 2008, the overall objective of the IASC Task Force on Climate Change is to promote the integration of climate change adaptation into humanitarian action and to ensure that, where appropriate, agency technical expertise and analysis can support Member State decision making within the UN's Framework Convention on Climate Change process.

Intergovernmental Panel on Climate Change (IPCC)

IPCC Secretariat c/o World Meteorological Organization
Geneva 2, Switzerland   CH-1211
+41-22-730-8208/84 • fax: +41-22-730-8025/13
email: IPCC-Sec@wmo.int
website: www.ipcc.ch

The IPCC was set up by the World Meteorological Organization and the United Nations Environment Programme. The role of the IPCC is to provide decision makers and others interested in climate change with an objective source of information about climate change. The site includes IPCC reports, press information, graphics, and speeches.

TreeHugger

website: www.treehugger.com

TreeHugger is dedicated to driving sustainability mainstream. Its website has a great deal of information about green news, solutions, and product information conveyed through blogs, daily and weekly newsletters, a radio show, and video segments.

US Environmental Protection Agency (EPA)
Climate Change Division

Ariel Rios Building, 1200 Pennsylvania Ave., NW
Washington, DC   20460
(202) 343-9990
website: www.epa.gov/climatechange

The website of the EPA's Climate Change Division offers comprehensive information on the issue of climate change in a way that is accessible and meaningful to all parts of society—communities, individuals, business, states and localities, and governments. The site offers a range of information on policies, science, health and environmental effects and actions individuals can take.

Bibliography

Books

Harold Ambler   *Don't Sell Your Coat: Surprising Truths About Climate Change.* East Lansing, MI: Lansing International Books, 2011.

Larry Bell   *Climate of Corruption: Politics and Power Behind the Global Warming Hoax.* Austin, TX: Greenleaf Book Group, 2011.

Lester R. Brown   *World on the Edge: How to Prevent Environmental and Economic Collapse.* New York: W.W. Norton & Company, 2011.

Paul Gilding   *The Great Disruption: Why the Climate Crisis Will Bring On the End of Shopping and the Birth of a New World.* New York: Bloomsbury Press, 2011.

Daniel Goleman   *Ecological Intelligence: How Knowing the Hidden Impacts of What We Buy Can Change Everything.* New York: Broadway Books, 2009.

Steve Goreham   *Climatism!: Science, Common Sense, and the 21st Century's Hottest Topic.* New Lenox, IL: New Lenox Books, 2010.

James Hansen   *Storms of My Grandchildren: The Truth About the Coming Climate Catastrophe and Our Last Chance to Save Humanity.* New York: Bloomsbury USA, 2009.

Richard Heinberg and Daniel Lerch, eds.   *The Post Carbon Reader: Managing the 21st Century's Sustainability Crises.* Healdsburg, CA: Watershed Media, 2010.

James Inhofe   *The Greatest Hoax: How the Global Warming Conspiracy Threatens Your Future.* Washington, DC: WND Press, 2012.

Matthew E. Kahn   *Climatopolis: How Our Cities Will Thrive in a Hotter Future.* New York: Basic Books, 2010.

Bill McKibben   *Earth: Making a Life on a Tough New Planet.* New York: Henry Holt and Company, 2010.

Patrick J. Michaels and Robert, Jr. Balling   *Climate of Extremes: Global Warming Science They Don't Want You to Know.* Washington, DC: Cato Institute, 2009.

A.W. Montford   *The Hockey Stick Illusion: Climategate and the Corruption of Science.* London, UK: Stacey International, 2010.

Thomas Gale Moore   *Global Warming: A Boon to Humans and Other Animals.* Stanford, CA: Hoover Institution on War, Revolution and Peace, 1995.

Joe Romm   *Hell and High Water: Global
                     Warming—the Solution and the
                     Politics—and What We Should Do.*
                     New York: HarperCollins, 2007.

Gernot Wagner   *But Will the Planet Notice?: How
                     Smart Economics Can Save the World.*
                     New York: Hill and Wang, 2011.

Periodicals and Internet Sources

Sharon Begley   "Are You Ready for More?," *Daily
                     Beast,* May 29, 2011.

Kiera Butler   "Should We Move Creatures
                     Threatened by Climate Change?,"
                     Mother Jones, January/February 2012.

Eileen Claussen   "Climate Change and the Economy:
                     Why Warnings Of Economic Doom
                     Are Overblown," *Building Operating
                     Management,* June 2009.

Down to Earth   "What Equals Effective," December
                     15, 2007.

The Economist   "Adapting to Climate Change: Facing
                     the Consequences," November 25,
                     2010.

Paul Epstein   "Food Security and Climate Change:
                     The True Cost of Carbon," *The
                     Atlantic,* September 27, 2011.

GRAIN   "Food and Climate Change: The
                     Forgotten Link," *Against the Grain,*
                     September 28, 2011.

Kenneth P. Green   "Who Should 'Go First' on
                      Greenhouse Gas Control?," *The
                      American*, April 17, 2009.

Anne Jolis   "Omitted: The Bright Side of Global
                      Warming," *Wall Street Journal*,
                      February 1, 2010.

Andrew E.   "Arctic Shortcut Beckons Shippers as
Kramer and   Ice Thaws," *New York Times*,
Andrew C. Revkin   September 10, 2009.

Eva Ludi   "Climate Change, Water, and Food
                      Security," *ODI Background Notes*,
                      March 2009.

Kari Manlove   "Helping Vulnerable Countries Adapt
                      to Global Warming,"
                      americanprogress.org, April 27, 2009.

Tara G. Martin   "Relocating Species to Ensure
and Eve   Survival in a Changing Climate,"
McDonald-   *Issues*, March 2011.
Madden

National Science   "Can Evolution Outplace Climate
Foundation   Change," *US News & World Report*,
                      June 13, 2011.

Brian Palmer   "Global Warming Would Harm the
                      Earth, but Some Areas Might Find It
                      Beneficial," *Washington Post*, January
                      23, 2011.

Roger Pielke Jr.,   "Lifting the Taboo on Adaptation,"
Gwyn Prins,   *Nature*, February 2007.
Steve Rayner, and
Daniel Sarewitz.

Graham Readfern "Preparing to Adapt to Unavoidable
Climate Change," *Ecos*, April–May
2010.

Anup Shah "Climate and Justice Equality,"
globalissues.org, January 8, 2012.

Philip Stevens "Poverty: The Real Threat to Health,"
africanliberty.org, May 15, 2009.

Alan Zarembo "Climate Change: Just Deal With It?"
Los Angeles Times, March 26, 2008.

Index

A

Acidification, oceans, 53
Adaptation
  business opportunities, 74–80
  mitigation is more important
    than, 51–57
  monetary costs, 63–64, 65, 72
  more important than mitiga-
    tion, 42–50
  must prioritize food security,
    96–106
  as politically incorrect, 43–44,
    46–47
  required for survival, due to
    climate change, 10–15, 88–89
  water system changes, 47, 85,
    88–89
"Adaptation trap," 52
"Adapting for a Green Economy:
  Companies, Communities and
  Climate Change" (report), 76–77
Adaptive capacity, 32–33, 49, 97–
  98, 103
Advertising
  anti-environmental, 76
  green businesses, 83
Africa
  agriculture, 29, 61, 89, 90
  business investment, 78
  central continent lack of
    changes, 26
  global warming's economic
    harms, 59
  health and disease, 13, 30, 60
  specific climate change effects,
    12, 13, 14, 29, 86, 87–88
  world water use, 89

African Water Week, 89
Agriculture
  adaptation and improvement
    measures, 15, 100–101, 105
  complex relationship with
    climate change, 89–90
  greenhouse gas emission rates,
    and, 62, 90
  production increases at higher
    latitudes, 27, 34, 46, 90
  seed varieties, 62, 101
  vulnerability, and food insecu-
    rity, 10, 12, 13, 14, 29, 30,
    58–59, 61, 62, 87, 98–99,
    100–101
Alfred Wegener Institute for Polar
  and Marine Research, 20–21
Algal blooms, 29
Andes, glacial melts, 14, 21, 30, 91
Animal adaptation examples, 45
Animal extinctions, 12, 37, 38–39,
  40, 53
Animal migration, 36–41
Antarctic ice melts, 21
Anthropomorphic climate change.
  See Human-caused climate
  change
*An Appeal to Reason: A Cool Look
  at Global Warming* (Lawson), 43
Architecture, climate change adap-
  tation, 47–48
Arctic ice melts
  benefits named, 27
  data/described, 11
  quick rates of melting, 21
Argentina, 73
Arnall, Sophie, 41

extent of human-caused, 11,
52–54
fertilization effect, 34
increase rates, 53
political protocols, plans, and
non-action, 42, 59, 63–64,
65, 68–69
taxation, 43
Greenland ice melt, 21
Greenpeace, 82, 84
"Greenwashing," 9, 81
Group of 77, 73
Guinea, desertification, 12
Gulf Coast, US, 79
See also Hurricane Katrina
(2005)

H

Habitat relocations, animals,
37–41
Hailes, Julia, 8
Haiti, 2010 earthquake, 49
Hamburg, Germany, 22
Harvard University, climate con-
ferences, 22–23
Health problems
climate change and disease,
15, 29–30, 75
disease and malnutrition, 29–
30, 88, 96–97, 98
vulnerability of poor nations,
13, 60–61
Heat-related deaths, 10, 12, 13, 46
Himalayas, glacial melts, 19, 21, 91
Holdren, John, 53
Homeless, US, 31–32
Honduras, 60
Hughes, Lesley, 38–39

Human-caused climate change
debated/doubted, 16–17,
46–47
described, 10–11, 14
effects on animals, 36
Human Development Index (UN),
49
Human migration. *See* Population
relocation/migration
Hunger and malnutrition, 30, 88,
96–97, 98, 99, 103, 104
Hurricane Andrew (1992), 33
Hurricane Katrina (2005), 22, 31–
32, 48, 53
Hurricane Mitch (1998), 60
Hurricane Rita (2005), 31–32
Hurricanes
climate change-related, 11,
13–14, 22, 31–32, 79–80
as climate events, 28, 31–32,
56
energy investment, hurricane
areas, 79
not climate change-related, 16,
23–24
Hydrologic cycle, 61
Hydropower, 14, 87, 89

I

Ice melts. *See* Arctic ice melts;
Glacial melts
Imports, food, 90, 95
India
agriculture, 62, 91
economic growth, and emissions, 48, 82
emissions reductions, 72
global warming's economic
harms, 59
heat, 13

CPSIA information can be obtained
at www.ICGtesting.com
Printed in the USA
FFOW021737261112

9 780737 761429